WHAT
SCARES
DEMONS?

SAM CHESS

WHAT SCARES DEMONS?

Published by:

UPWARD! Ministries LLC
P.O. Box 880263
Port Saint Lucie, Florida 34988

First Printing – August 2021
Printed in the United States of America

***ISBN PDF:* 978-0-9997977-3-0**

This book is dedicated to Dr. Walter B. Barron.

He's the reason it was written.

You will learn more of our story as you read.

CONTENTS

WHAT SCARES DEMONS:
Part I

I had an unusually potent experience the summer of 2020. I was out walking around a lake near my home. God began to speak to me in a very powerful way.

When I got back to my truck, I grabbed a pad of paper and began to write as fast as my pen would move. Every time I finished a sentence, another was waiting to be written, page after page after page!

This book is the result of what God revealed to me on those scrawled pages.

Introduction

Only six people in the entire Old Testament were healed or revived from the dead!

Six people! Surprised? However when Jesus' public ministry begins in the New Testament Gospels, there is an explosion of the Messiah healing huge numbers of sick and diseased people. Miraculously! People who had totally given up on life became whole again. Why? What was the point?

In the first century world where hospitals and medical help for the common and the poor people simply didn't exist, suddenly, one man appears and starts restoring unmoving, pain-ridden, rotting bodies to complete health, with just a word from his mouth or a touch from his hand! And it wasn't just the few people who are specifically detailed in Scripture, both Matthew and Luke in their Gospels stress that he healed **all the sick** who were brought to him. *(Matthew 4:23, 9:35; Luke 4:40)*

Huge crowds would surround Jesus with their lifelong illnesses and he healed them all – whole villages, whole regions. You couldn't walk anywhere, particularly around the region of Galilee, without finding somebody who had been miraculously made whole by Jesus! Everybody knew somebody!

What is equally stunning is that even with those numbers stacking up, religious leaders, particularly the Pharisees, and then a growing group of the common people rejected Jesus! They hated him, plotted his death, and finally executed this Healer who was clearly doing many, many times more supernatural miracles than any human had ever done before *(including all the greatest of the Old Testament prophets combined)!*

"He needs to die," they said! "He is a blasphemer because he claims to be God here on this earth, here to redeem us from our sins!"

- Even though we have been intently expecting our long-awaited Messiah,
- Even though this man fulfills every Messianic prophecy we have been teaching people our whole lives,
- Even though this man is daily doing things only God could possibly do,
- We want him dead, because <u>he is telling us that we are sinners and that we need to repent</u> of our sins!

Jesus' miraculous healings were undoubtedly meant to **prove that he was God** in human form. They did!

But there is a **<u>second proof of Jesus' divinity</u>** that goes far deeper than all those thousands of healed bodies. That is:

The casting of demons out of the demon possessed!

In the proving of Jesus' Divinity, in Jesus' attempt to convince people that he was the Messiah, and that the Messiah on this earth was indeed incarnate God; in proving that HE was the same "Mighty God, the Everlasting Father" that Isaiah had prophesied *(Isaiah 9:6)*; in proving to people that he was Mighty God in flesh – here on this earth to solve humanity's unsolvable 'sin-curse' problem; in accomplishing all of that;

The miracle of casting demons out of people was far more potent than even the restoring of missing legs, or the resurrecting of the dead back to life!

Are you with me? Let's dig in a step deeper:

- ✓ How many demon-possessed people do we find in the Old Testament?   Zero!

- ✓ How many demon-possessed people do we find in the Epistles?   Zero!

Is that a shocking discovery? That's not to say that satan and his fallen minions weren't here on this earth tempting people to do very sinful things during those times. Clearly the 'devil' was working his evil starting with Adam and Eve, and without question humanity did a lot of very wicked things throughout the first 2/3's of the Bible.

Revelation 12 gives us a flashback to the beginning of time and it shows us 1/3 of God's angels rebelling and falling with satan to this earth. *(Revelation 12:7-9, Luke 10:18)*

So demons – fallen angels, were already here from the time of Adam, and they were already working their evil schemes to thwart God's great redemptive plan.

They are the ones who made the Pharisees so hate Jesus! They convinced the very people who had seen Jesus healing so many sick, perhaps even their own relatives, to finally scream "Crucify him"!

But why were so many demon-possessed people suddenly showing up everywhere just as Jesus started his preaching? Did "demon possession" only happen during Jesus' three year ministry on this earth? No... certainly not! Were people "possessed" by demons in Old Testament times? Of course! *(We just don't specifically read about them.)*

- It would be hard to look at somebody like Assyrian King Sennacharib in Nineveh who cut off thousands of people's heads and piled them up in pyramids and drove poles through people's bodies which he hung up as ornaments around the city, and not say he was completely under the control of satan and his fallen angels! Right? Without question!

- Were their demon possessed-people during the times of the Epistles? And are there still evil demon-possessed people on this earth today? Yes, without doubt!

One of the most vivid memories from my boyhood years was watching an out-of-control, demon-possessed man being wrestled to the floor by the men in my church. I watched with bulging eyes, I'm sure, as the older people in the church prayed *(and young Sammy prayed too)* until the demon came out and the man was forgiven, cleansed, and in his right mind.

I've designed the first few chapters of this book to show us vividly the absolute power Jesus demonstrated over satan and his demons during his three year earthly ministry.

That's what the first century onlookers were seeing, that's what the Pharisees couldn't miss. If Jesus was doing an amazing thing in healing thousands of sick people, *(something they had never seen done before)*, imagine how much more powerful it was for him to be freeing people who had been chained under the unbreakable bondage of satan?

A single sentence in Gadara and a "maniac" that had been terrorizing the whole region became a "missionary." That had to be powerful! Attention grabbing!

And yet many of the people who watched all that power, still rejected Jesus! *(We'll see that often in the pages ahead.)*

So, let me take us on a logical **(theo-logical,** *theos-logos,* **God-logic/reason)** path here as we take a hard, systematic biblical look at the satanic, the demonic.

- It is imperative that I not go one word beyond what the Bible teaches on this subject!

- But it is also just as important that I unfold everything the Bible does teach, because it so deeply affects our daily spiritual life!

I have a Pastor in the next town north of me that became a dear friend. His name is Walter Barron. I often called him and we prayed together. I called him to pray with me on the life-changing 'walk around the lake' that I mentioned on page 7. His prayer set off a chain of events that led to the writing of this book.

He said something, then prayed something that rattled my cage. It led me to determine that I would make sure I truly knew what the Bible teaches on this subject and how that truth should apply to my life! *(I'll soon refer back to his prayer.)*

I began to call on God and push back against the forces of darkness during that walk around the lake like I never had before. When I got back to my truck, I grabbed a pad of paper and began to write as fast as my pen would move…

Chapter 1

"The Scripture you've just heard has been fulfilled…"

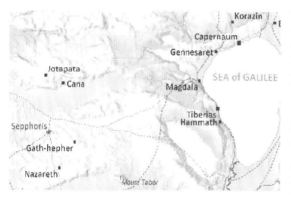

You remember that Jesus grew up in the village of Nazareth. He probably *(IMO)* worked with Joseph in the construction of the new **Roman City of "Sepphoris"** that Herod the Great's son, Antipas, commissioned to be built just three miles northwest of Nazareth, four miles southwest of Cana. Herod's new "Jewel of Galilee," capital city was being built at exactly the time Jesus was in his adolescence, teen years, and 20's. The ruins are still there today. Imagine Jesus in that new growing city as an incredible, sought-after woodcraftsman! *(IMO = 'in my opinion' throughout this book.)*

Jesus shocked his whole town one day by putting down his tools, walking into the synagogue in Nazareth on the Sabbath, stepping up to the podium, opening up the scroll to Isaiah 61, and reading a prophecy that had undoubtedly been written about the long-awaited coming Messiah:

Luke 4:18-21: '"The Spirit of the LORD is upon me, for he has anointed me to bring Good News to the poor. He has sent me to proclaim that captives will be released, that the blind will see, that the oppressed will be set free, and that the time of the LORD's favor has come.' He rolled up the scroll, handed it back to the attendant, and sat down. All eyes in the synagogue looked at him intently. Then he began to speak to them. 'The Scripture you've just heard has been fulfilled this very day!'"

He was clearly announcing that he was/is the Messiah! Some people today say Jesus kept his divinity under wraps. That's not true!

- But there wasn't a single person listening that day that didn't understand exactly what Jesus was proclaiming!
- Remember the very next thing that happened – his own town's people tried to kill him, by throwing him off a cliff!
- That's when he packed his suitcase and moved twelve miles northeast to Capernaum, where Peter and Andrew, James and John lived. *(Matthew 4:13)*

But, notice the words that Jesus quoted in the Nazareth synagogue that day:

1) The Spirit has anointed me to bring the Gospel to the poor. (πτωχος) The surface meaning is not having much money, the deeper Biblical meaning is "the poor in spirit" who know they need a Savior!

2) The Spirit has sent me to set captives free! What captives – Who's bound by whom?

3) To cause blind people not to be blind anymore. Physical blindness? No! Even when Jesus healed the "man born blind" it was primarily to point everyone to their own spiritual blindness!

4) The Spirit has sent me to set the oppressed free. What oppressed? Who are the "freed" oppressed?

Some "socially-focused" Bible students will stress that Jesus was talking about poor people who are being downtrodden by society around them. And Jesus was promising to "set the oppressed free"!

But remember, Jesus is saying this at a time when everyone he was talking to was under the oppression of the Roman Government. People in that day thought he was promising to free them from Rome's rule. He wasn't! He ended up dying at the hand of Roman soldiers to free people from what was really eternally "oppressing" them:

The sin chains that satan had on their souls, binding up all of their lives!

Notice, satan and his evil minions are there when Jesus quotes Isaiah 61 and declares himself to be the Messiah. They are the ones who inspired the town's people to try to kill him!

I'm sure there must have been some kind of emergency meeting in the conference room of satan and his demons, because they knew very well who the Isaiah 61 "poor" were.

They knew exactly who the "captives and oppressed" were that Jesus came to set free. **They were the captors!**

They were the "oppressors" of the souls of humanity. They knew all about spiritual blindness. **They were the ones causing it!**

 I've purposely included a clipart image of a demon. I have no idea if this is what a demon really looks like, and it doesn't matter because of what I'm getting ready to tell you. I put it in here for two reasons:

In today's world of special effects, fantasy in movies, and video games, this kind of image is available at the punch of a button to a 5-year-old kid. It's easy to dismiss this kind of thing as pure fantasy and **imagine that the largely invisible world of evil around us doesn't exist. It does!**

If you believe in the devil and demons, you can look at this image and shudder over the horrible effects a thousand of these creatures could have on your life, or the lives of your children or grandchildren. That's also bad theology!

- I am going to show you something I never saw before writing this book.
- Remember I can only take this as far as Scripture takes it...
- But I must take it every bit as far as the Bible unfolds the topic!

Jesus' primary task on this earth was to die to pay the sin penalty of the world so that we could be forgiven and cleansed from our many sins. When Jesus was asked why he was here, he said those very words:

> **Luke 19:10: "For the Son of Man has come to seek and to save those who are lost."**
>
> **John 3:16-17: "For God so loved the world that he gave his one and only Son, that whoever believes in him shall not perish but have eternal life. For God did not send his Son into the world to condemn the world, but to save the world through him."**

So, that's what he came to do for us, in a positive way, as a Savior, as the Savior, as **OUR SAVIOR**! But in a powerful, negative *(for them)* way Jesus also came as a **HEAVENLY WARRIOR** to do fatal damage to the "kingdom of darkness"!

> **Hebrews 2:14-15: "Since the children have flesh and blood, he too shared in their humanity so that by his death he might break the power of him who holds the power of death—that is, the devil—and free those who all their lives were held in slavery by their fear of death."**

- Jesus didn't come to this earth to have a word spat with satan. He came to destroy him!

- Jesus' death didn't just pay your sin penalty – it put a divine eternal dagger into satan's sin-blackened heart!

1 John 3:8: "But when people keep on sinning, it shows that they belong to the devil, who has been sinning since the beginning. *(That's what Jesus was trying to get the Pharisees to understand.)* **But the Son of God came to DESTROY the works of the devil."**

We look around us in modern times and see sheer evil seemingly winning over and over again. Then we turn back to Scripture and read these passages about Jesus' defeat of satan and sometimes *(to be absolutely honest)* something kind of backfires in our minds.

- Some of you reading this have been going through personal events that you know for certain have a "spiritual warfare" component.

- And you have spent days, even the last few weeks, feeling like you were in hand-to-hand combat with the evil one and his minions! *(You probably were!)*

- And you have felt like you are spiritually bloodied and battered, always retreating, while you timidly hold up your shield of faith trying to stave off "the fiery darts of the evil one"! *(Ephesians 6:16)*

- **So if satan was destroyed by the death of Jesus on the cross, how in the world does he seem to be so effective in inserting himself into your life, your marriage, your finances, your children's lives, and your grand-children's lives?** *(and on and on…)*

- I've preached often about how satan's power in the life of a Believer has been ripped away by

Jesus' victory on the cross – yet he still continues to come after us with accusations, false information, temptations to slip off the path, and manipulations that we should see right through, but often do not. Doesn't he?

> **"Submit yourselves therefore to God. Resist the devil, and he will flee from you."**
> James 4:7 (KJV)

Doesn't James 4:7 clearly say that **if we submit ourselves to God and resist satan, he will be forced to flee?**

- Didn't this Jesus come "to set the captives free,"
- And once he set us free, didn't he plant the same Holy Spirit in us that He said was "on him" – so that those who were blind would not be blind anymore, and those who were oppressed by the chains of satan would be set free from his bondage and power!
- **Isn't that talking about us**?

Haven't we been set free? Aren't we now infused to the depths of our soul with the same Spirit who in-filled and empowered Jesus on that very day he said he came to offer freedom to those who were bound by satan?

Freedom from captivity – freedom from oppression – freedom from spiritual blindness!

One of the startling things about that day when I prayed with my Pastor friend, Walter, was that he just launched into a rather forceful conversation with satan. He wasn't being nice. He wasn't trying to be polite.

He detailed to satan what Scripture says he could and could not do, **and I was listening, thinking... "Well, why in the world not!"** *(Remember again, we can't practice anything more than what the Bible says, but we should be willing to practice every single thing that the Bible teaches!)*

My friend told satan what was acceptable and then in no uncertain terms he told satan what was not acceptable! Then he called on the power of Jesus' death and resurrection on our behalf to enforce a protective wall around us and our families.

Is that really what a Christian is supposed to do?

Aren't we instead supposed to back ourselves into the corner, hold up our protective "shield of faith" *(Ephesians 6:16)* and pray like crazy that none of satan's fiery darts get through?

In this task of being soldiers in the Lord's army, are we supposed to be <u>**defensive**</u> soldiers just trying to hold the fort against a strong and vicious enemy, or are we supposed to be <u>**offensive**</u> soldiers, who pick up the Sword of the Spirit and start doing some damaging eternal slicing and dicing?

And for all who are in places of Spiritual leadership as Generals or Colonels or Lieutenants in the Lord's army, at what point do you lift your sword, yell "charge," and <u>run right toward the enemy</u>?

- "But Sam, satan is so strong, his demons are so powerful!" **<u>Are they</u>?** Are you sure?

- But look at what they are doing to the sinful world around us! Yes! **But you are not actually** *(biblically)* **part of the sinful world around you**!

- "Oh, but Sam, I'm so spiritually weak, I'm so easily tripped up!"

- Listen to me: If you are a Believer – **You are one of God's Redeemed! You are one of God's Saints! You are Jesus' Church! That changes everything for you!**

1 John 5:18-19: "We know that God's children do not make a practice of sinning, for God's Son holds them securely, <u>and the evil one cannot touch them</u>. We know that <u>we are children of God</u> and that the world around us is under the control of the evil one." *(Notice "the world around us" vs. "God's children.")*

There is a very strong line drawn in Scripture between what satan is still allowed to get away with *(That allowance will one day come to a crashing halt!)* – there is a line between what he can get away with for those who have no commitment to Jesus as Lord and Savior, and a very different strong line of what he can't get away with for those who have committed their lives and their eternal futures to Jesus!

Colossians 1:12-14: "He has enabled you to share in the inheritance that belongs to his people, who live in the light. For he has rescued us from the kingdom of darkness and transferred us into the Kingdom of his dear Son, who purchased our freedom and forgave our sins."

- Satan can't bind you with his chains anymore! If he's still doing it, he's doing it through fraud, deceit, and manipulation. Many Christians keep on sinning because they don't realize the awesome power over sin and satan that has been unleashed in their lives!

- If you could see inside the minds of satan and his minions right now *(IMO)* it would look very different than what we tend to think. Let me show you a powerful truth:

In Luke chapter four, once Jesus has declared himself to be the long-awaited Messiah, who is here to release captives and set the oppressed free – He, as we said, packed his bags, moved to Capernaum, and immediately had a run in with a demon-possessed man. Does anybody think that was accidental?

What we get to see when Jesus, our Savior and Lord, runs into demons should change our whole attitude toward satan!

As we said, demons were undoubtedly present in the Old Testament, but they stayed under the radar where overt demon activity tends to try to stay.

- They don't want you to watch the actions of sinful humanity and associate it with them! They want you to think the sinful person is just "expressing their individuality."
- Everybody should be able to do any action they want, and no one else should judge them! Demons don't want anybody to see their level of control!

But when Jesus arrives on the scene and starts preaching the truths of God, the demons can't stand it, they can't stay hidden. They scream out of the people they are possessing, not once, but on several occasions.

What we see and hear from demons when they scream out in Scripture, should make you never fear them again in your life because the actual truth is – **demons are scared to death of your God and they are scared to death of YOU, a Redeemed Saint, and the presence of God that lives in you!**

"You believe that there is one God. Good! Even the demons believe that—and they tremble/shudder (φρίσσω) in terror!" (James 2:19)

Any mental picture of demons strutting around the universe flashing obscene gestures in God's direction doesn't appear to be accurate.

Every single time demons come in contact with Jesus in the Bible, they are clearly scared out of their minds! And that also seems to extend to Jesus' Redeemed Children when they are truly operating in the awesome power of God within them!

- Please hear me on this: Any of you who have received Jesus' sin payment freeing you from the dominion of darkness – the idea that you need to be cowering before the enemy of your soul in fear is a lie from the pit of hell! That is not what is presented in Scripture at all!

- Satan and his minions can appear very powerful when they are dealing with unregenerate people. But the moment they run into a Redeemed Saint, I promise you everything changes for them!

Luke 4:31-34: "Then Jesus went to Capernaum, a town in Galilee, and taught there in the synagogue every Sabbath day. There, too, the people were amazed at his teaching, for he spoke with authority. Once when he was in the synagogue, a man possessed by a demon—an evil spirit cried out, shouting, 'Go away! Why are you interfering with us, Jesus of Nazareth? Have you come to destroy us? I know who you are—the Holy One of God!'"

The demons knew exactly who Jesus was! How?

- Because they had been in heaven with him before the rebellion! They had at one time worshipped him as the God of the universe! It was God's creation of the "in his image" human beings that had apparently ticked them off enough to rebel! *(IMO)*

- When Jesus arrived on earth in human form, <u>it struck terror to their hearts</u>!

- They knew a divine plan was now in place that would certainly smash their little evil kingdom into oblivion!

- When Jesus began to preach about dying for the sins of the world, then rising from the dead, few of the humans seemed to catch on, but <u>you can bet the demons did</u>!

- When Jesus spoke in Nazareth about freeing the captives, the oppressed, and making the spiritually blind see, satan and his minions knew exactly who he was talking about!

There's every reason to assume that when Jesus started preaching in Capernaum, he might have used the same Isaiah 61 text that he had used back in Nazareth. And part way through his message a demon couldn't take the heat anymore, and he screamed out in terror:

Luke 4:33-34: "'Go Away! Why are you attacking me? Why are you attacking us? Have you come to destroy us? I know who you are, the Holy One of God!'" *(You are the Incarnate Messiah – the Christ!)*

We'll soon look at another demoniac in Luke 8. We'll find the same terror and similar words: **"<u>I beg you not to torment me</u>."** The demons knew that the Almighty had arrived on earth in human form when they heard Jesus preaching!

And to make the situation even more spine-chilling for them,

- Jesus purposely jammed in their evil faces news of an ever-lasting fire he'd "prepared for the devil and his angels!" *(Matthew 25:41)*

- And when satan and his demons would finally get their first read of the book of Revelation, they would know their final destiny! They were/are going to end up forever in a "lake of fire"!

- Jesus' Redeemed Saints, on the other hand, are going to end up forever in Heaven in the presence of their loving Heavenly Father!

- If that double truth doesn't particularly excite you now, I can assure you: **It terrifies satan and his demons!**

Jesus set out to prove unconditionally – over and over that he had 100% control over the satanic and the demonic!

Luke 4:35: "But Jesus reprimanded him. 'Be quiet! Come out of the man,' he ordered. At that, the demon threw the man to the floor as the crowd watched; then it came out of him without hurting him further."

Let me just say this early in this book: If satan seems to have his guns trained on you, it should alert you, as to how seriously he is taking you! You are *(or he sees you can become)* a threat to his evil kingdom!

Satan actually fears the son or daughter of God, particularly when you open your mouth and proclaim the truth of God's Word!

- What satan's demons are trying to do in your life, they are doing in panicked desperation! They are frantically trying to stave off the inevitable!

- The demons are sweating bullets, like somebody who is drowning and reaching out to pull under the person nearest them.

- When we, as Believers, feel fear and desperation in our lives, it is because we are allowing them to drag us into their terror!

- Satan's minions have no (legal) right to do that to you!

They have <u>no real power</u> over you,
the Redeemed Believer!

———————

They know something that they hope you never find out:

1) They know that all the power is on your side! **You are a Son or Daughter of the Most, High God!**

2) And they are scared to death of what you will do with your life when you figure that out!

Chapter 2

*So the long-awaited, long-prophesied Messiah,
God incarnate, shows up on this planet!*

Nobody on the earth *(except perhaps his mother Mary)* knows who Jesus really is. They should have, they had been expecting him, they had lots of prophesies!

The prophet Isaiah clearly said the Messiah would be Mighty God, Everlasting Father and that his divine rule would be an "everlasting rule." But first he would have to arrive as a human baby. *(Isaiah 9:6-7)* None of these were hidden prophesies. Every Jewish kid learned them on their parent's lap.

So what had to happen to convince the world that He, Jesus *(the carpenter's son)*, was the promised incarnate God of the universe? And that he was now here on this earth to redeem his beloved children from their sentence of eternal punishment, and offer them forgiveness, soul cleansing, and eternal life?

- What did Jesus need to do to convince them?
- Does the Bible lay out all the evidence they *(or we)* need to believe in him? Yes? No?

1) He had to fulfill every Old Testament prophesy written over 4,000 years without missing one test. He did!

2) He had to be born into the right nation, the right lineage, the exact right family. He amazingly had to be born to a virgin girl in that family. He was!

3) He had to be able to demonstrate his power over the physical world as only the Creator God can do. He had to have power over the wind and water and the growth of trees. He did!

4) More importantly he had to have power over sickness and disease. And we've already discussed how Jesus healed thousands and thousands of hopeless people. That was something no one had ever seen anybody do before.

5) He even had to have power over life and death. He needed to raise dead people back to life again – and he did!

I'm scaling up here more and more:

6) If Jesus was truly the God of heaven, if he was the Messiah Savior that Daniel and Isaiah had prophesied, he must have the power to forgive people's sins and set them free from sin's shackles. He would have to be able to take the most sin-blackened heart and so radically transform them that they became a brand new person – and he did!

And he is still doing that today! He has done that very same thing in so many of us reading this!

7) But there is one more thing that the Messiah Savior had to accomplish to prove to the world that **he was who he said he was:** If Jesus was the true Messiah – he would have to demonstrate power over satan, power over demons! <u>He did!</u>

Compare these two verses:

> **1 John 5:19: "We know that we are children of God, and that the whole world is <u>under the control of the evil one</u>."** *(Notice the contrast: God's children vs. the whole world under the evil one's control.)*

> **Ephesians 2:1-2: "You were dead in the trespasses and sins in which you once walked, following the course of this world, following <u>the prince of the power of the air</u>, the spirit that is now at work in the sons of disobedience."**

Do you see the contrast? Satan is in control *(for now)* in this "world" and over its sin-cursed people. But there is a second category of people on the other side of the line who satan and his minions can't/shouldn't/don't have any right **to control at all – that's the children of God! You!**

Let's add in a second line up of Scriptures that will begin to obliterate the "we're all under the control of the evil one" theme:

These verses are really important: We'll soon come to the famous account of a man possessed by as many as 6,000 demons! But we first need to get these "we're on the other side" verses etched into our minds:

John 12:31: "The time for judging this world has come, when Satan, <u>the ruler of this world, will be cast out</u>."

John 16:10-11: "Righteousness is available because I go to the Father, and you will see me no more. Judgment will come <u>because the ruler of this world has already been judged</u>."

Colossians 2:15: *(As Jesus' blood is pouring down the cross for your sins and mine.)* "He <u>disarmed</u> the *(demonic)* <u>powers and authorities</u>, he made a public spectacle of them, triumphing over them by the cross."

Hebrews 2:14: "Since the children have flesh and blood, he too shared in their humanity so that <u>by his death he might break the power of him who holds the power of death—that is, the devil!</u>"

Romans 16:20: *(To the Roman Believers who were being hounded and persecuted.)* "The God of peace will <u>soon crush Satan under your feet</u>. May the grace of our Lord Jesus be with you." Turns out:

Jesus didn't just come to save us from sin!
He also came to save us <u>from satan</u>!

- Jesus certainly did come to save us from the bondage of our sins!
- He did come to save us from a godless death!
- He did come to save us from judgment and hell!

- But he also specifically came to snatch us from the chains of the "ruler of this world" and set us free! *(John 12:31-33)*
- He came to "destroy the works of the devil" in human lives! *(I John 3:8)*
- He came to "break the power of the devil, who holds/held the power of spiritual, physical, and eternal death!" *(Hebrews 2:14)*
- He came to crush satan under his feet *(as God promised Eve in Genesis 3:15).*
- He came to crush satan, not just under his feet, but under your feet as well! *(Romans 16:20)* Those are not my words, they are God's words!

Let me take us through a **seven-point theology** here. If we do not grasp this, we will not understand why Jesus came to earth at all!

1) When God created humans in his image, Genesis 1:26 says he gave them "<u>dominion</u>" over the earth. Psalm 8:6 says God put everything under Adam and Eve's feet *(including apparently, satan and his rebellious fallen angels).*

2) When satan goes after Adam and Eve, he's not just gunning for their fall, <u>he's going after the ruler-ship of the world</u> that God gave them!

3) If Adam and Eve rebel and transfer their allegiance to satan, the "dominion" of the earth slips out of their hands into satan's. They did – and it did! *(That's why the Apostle Paul calls satan the "ruler of this world"! Do we see that?)*

33

4) In God's infinite "system of Divine justice" humanity had given away the ruler-ship he gave them, and humanity would be required to retrieve it. But… every single human was still locked under the chains of satan's bondage!

5) In order to justly reverse the effects of the fall, a man had to be born on earth who was not under the dominion of satan. **That "man" had to battle satan in a cosmic war that ended in the retrieval of the ruler-ship of this earth.** To wrestle humanity out from under satan's clutches, that "man" had to personally atone for humanity's sin. *(Does this make sense?)*

6) But how in the world could any sin-chained man be free of satan's bondage and have the power to take satan on one-on-one and beat him once and for all? **The only way that could possibly happen would be if God himself could somehow climb into a human body! He did!** In God's system of Divine justice this was Plan A – there was absolutely no Plan B!

7) When Jesus said "it is finished" without giving satan any claim on him, he had **pushed an unwitting satan into being a tool to bring about the very thing satan was trying not to do – lose his stranglehold on humanity.** A sinless substitute had finally and totally paid the sin price for every one of them. Satan lost his grip on the "dominion of the earth" – because now, person after person, (thousands, millions, billions of people) would be able to break completely free of the evil one's clutches!

The battle between Jesus and satan was so much bigger than we tend to think. It was even bigger than the once-in-a-while illustrations recorded in Scripture. But sometimes we get to look inside the cosmic struggle that was going on for our eternal souls and what we see is astounding.

I made some initial statements in the last chapter. Let's expand them a bit:

- What we get to see when Jesus, our Savior and Lord, runs into demons should change our whole attitude toward satan and his minions. In James 2:19: "Even the demons believe *(in who Jesus is)* and tremble/shudder *(φρίσσω- tremble in terror)."*

- What we see and hear when demons meet Jesus and scream out in Scripture, should make you never live in terror of them again in your life. Because **the actual truth is – demons are scared to death of your God! They are scared out of their mind of your Savior! And they are scared of YOU, a Redeemed Saint, because of the presence of God that lives within you!**

Let's prove that by unwrapping an amazing story in Scripture. This is without question the greatest demonic deliverance story in the Bible. If part of what Jesus needed to do to prove his divinity, his Messiah-ship was to show his power over the demonic, **then this is the big one!**

- His face-off with satan in the wilderness was a huge event, but only Jesus and satan were present to witness that one.
- Thousands of people are going to witness this account, and it is going to have reverberations that go on for generations. *(In fact, right up until today!)*

One day when Jesus asks a demon-possessed man what his name is, the voice that uses his voice box is a "demon spokesman." I say demon spokesman because "the voice" says that the demons living in the man were **"legion."** Legion is not a name, it's a number! In Roman times a legion of military soldiers was 6,000. Remember Mary Magdalene, the bad girl of Scripture? She had just seven demons possessing her, and her life was in complete shambles before Jesus delivered her.

The man in the Luke 8 story had as many as 6,000 demons literally living in his body! He was an insane maniac and had been for years. Not one thought, not one action were from his own rational mind. Every single reaction, every single word was controlled by any one or more of thousands of demons.

There were so many demons in him, they had a hierarchy of command, and one of them was appointed the "press secretary" when the man needed to say something.

> **Luke 8:26: "So they arrived in the region of the Gerasenes, across the lake from Galilee."**

(Don't get bothered over one Gospel writer calling it Gerasenes and one calling it Gadarenes. That was simply two different towns and the region went by the name of one of them, much like my own home town is Port Saint Lucie and our county is Saint Lucie County in Florida.)

Much more importantly, we need to know that the disciples left the western Jewish region of Galilee, *(surely)* not expecting to end up on the Southeast side of the Sea of Galilee. So what happened?

The Sea is 13 miles long *(700 feet below sea level),* and is hemmed in by mountains. In the last chapter we read that Jesus left Nazareth and went <u>down</u> to Capernaum even though he was traveling north. That was because the terrain drops 2,000 feet in 12 miles.

The problem was boaters could be minding their own business, trying to sail a half dozen miles down the coast, and a storm could suddenly appear over the mountains. They would find themselves *(without radar on their cell phones)* fighting for their lives. And, that's exactly what happened.

Luke 8:22: "One day Jesus said to his disciples, 'Let's cross to the other side of the lake.'" *(The crowds, looking for healing, were crushing against him every moment of every day.)* I seriously doubt that the disciples thought Jesus meant the "other side" of the lake *(northeast to southwest).* There is no evidence they ever went south to Gentile heathen Gadara often, or ever – until the later unexpected feeding of the 4,000. So, wherever the disciples thought they were sailing to, only Jesus knew where they were really going!

- There was a massive storm. Jesus was sleeping.
- The boat started to capsize. The seasoned-fishermen disciples screamed in fear.
- Jesus woke up, calmed the storm and said, "Where is your faith, guys?"
- They responded; "<u>Who in the world is this guy</u>? <u>Even the wind obeys him</u>!"

What we can be somewhat sure of is that they didn't intend to end up where they did *(at the base of a pagan graveyard)*, except for Jesus! He had a divine appointment!

Luke 8:27-28: "As Jesus was climbing out of the boat, a man who was possessed by demons came out to meet him. For a long time he had been homeless and naked, living in the tombs outside the town. As soon as he saw Jesus, he shrieked and fell down in front of him."

It's probably early dawn. Jesus stills the violent waves. The boat is full of water. They limp to the closest land. They are all amazed at what they had just seen take place and absolutely exhausted by the horrifying night they had endured. As they are climbing out of the boat soaked to the skin, here comes this screaming maniac *(two of them, Matthew 8 says.)*

Sixteen times we are told in the Gospels that somebody was controlled by a demon. This guy had a whole legion!

- He was naked. Mark 5 says that night and day he was hacking and gashing his body with sharp stones!

- Mark 5:3 says nobody could control him. The power of the demons was too strong! He and his evil buddy lived in the tombs among the dead. When anybody got near their territory, they would run with bloodcurdling, hellish screams toward them.

- One has to assume that if the demons in them caused them to harm themselves, unsuspecting people who strayed too close might have been injured or even killed as well.

- I'm going to assume that they had killed people. *(satan comes to kill, and destroy.)* Luke 8 says the town's people tried to "bind him up with chains" *(arrest him)*, but he would snap anything he was bound with, like twigs, and run back to the tombs.

That's who Jesus has chosen to confront! In a few minutes time, he is going to convert this man from the "kingdom of darkness" into the "kingdom of light."

He's going to **transform him from a demon-crazed maniac into a missionary**! He is going to show the whole region his complete, total, instant, supernatural authority over the most demons anyone has ever seen housed inside of one human being!

We all need to grasp this: We sometimes get the idea that in this battle between good and evil in our lives, we are caught in the middle between two equal opposing sides:

1) God, who we believe made the world – He has great power over it and in it.

2) An equally powerful satan – who constantly rages out of control in our lives and in the world around us.

That is not at all how the Bible presents the comparison between God and satan! The truth is, <u>satan and his demons are paralyzed with fear with one word from our Savior!</u>

Luke 8:28: "As soon as he saw Jesus, he shrieked and fell down in front of him. Then he screamed, 'Why are you interfering with me, Jesus, Son of the Most, High God? Please, I beg you, don't torture me!'"

Allow me to continue to re-insert these sentences. This is what God has been drilling into my mind, and I would like it to wash over your soul as well:

Demons are scared to death of your God!
They are scared out of their mind –
in the presence of your Savior!

In this account, all 6,000 of these demons are shivering and falling in terror at the very sight of Jesus. Remember, they knew exactly who Jesus was. They had at one time been worshipping him in heaven before their fall!

- In **Matthew 25:41,** as we said, Jesus refers to **the "ever-lasting fire" which was prepared for the devil and his angels.**

- My guess is that this is by no means the only time Jesus used that phrase. In this massive cosmic battle that Jesus waged for three earthly years for your eternal soul, he was constantly landing blow after blow on satan and his demons. <u>They knew</u>!

- You remember in satan's direct confrontation with Jesus in the wilderness, **he didn't say: "IF you are the Son of God," he said, "SINCE you are the Son of God"** turn these stones into bread! <u>He knew</u>!

- I don't have a single doubt that Jesus often repeated the phrase about the "eternal fire" that the demons were headed for! **They knew,** and they were *(and are)* living in terror! We get to see here that they are scared out of their minds of something called "THE ABYSS."

Luke 8:31: "The demons kept begging Jesus not to send them into the bottomless pit. (ἄβυσσος – *abussos - abyss)"*

When John writes Revelation 20, the third chapter from the end of the Bible, he writes of <u>a bottomless lake of fire</u>. And in no uncertain terms says that when Jesus returns, in his glorious Second Coming – he will lock satan in the abyss! *(Revelation 20:10-14)*

*The next time satan reminds you of your past,
remind him of his future!*

When you see satan raging around in this world, remember that right in the frontal lobe of his mind, **is what Jesus said is his coming, eternal future!**

I'm not trying to be a wise-guy, shaking my finger in the face of satan. We don't want to be somebody who is flippantly telling this demon to do this and commanding that demon to do that. Satan is a whole lot more powerful than any of us personally are. Don't even imagine trying to take him on in your own strength!

- But that is where our minds tend to do a hiccup.
- It's true that I'm as weak as water in the face of a very powerful adversary.
- **But one word from my Savior's mouth and that powerful adversary is turned into a quivering ball of terror!** *(Do we see that?)*

Luke 8:28-32: "As soon as he saw Jesus, he shrieked and fell down in front of him. Then he screamed, 'Why are you interfering with me, Jesus, Son of the Most, High God? Please, I beg you, don't torture me!' For Jesus had already commanded the evil spirit to come out of him. This spirit had often taken control of the man. Even when he was placed under guard and put in chains and shackles, he simply broke them and rushed out into the wilderness, completely under the demon's power.

Jesus demanded, 'What is your name'? 'Legion,' he replied, for he was filled with many demons. The demons kept begging Jesus not to send them into the bottomless pit. There happened to be a large herd of pigs feeding on the hillside nearby." We know there were 2,000 pigs in the herd and everyone of them were affected, so there had to be a minimum of 2000 demons and perhaps as many as 6,000 – three per pig. *(Mark 5:13)* As the old joke says: "<u>This was the first ever recorded incident of *deviled ham*</u>"!

- Every single one of the demons are terrorized and immobilized at the very sight of Jesus. Not a single one of them has enough power to lift the demonic man to his feet and have him attempt to grab Jesus around the neck.

- These demons knew from the moment God arrived in a human body that they were in for a cosmic war!

- Herod's earlier attempt to kill all the firstborn in Bethlehem was not hatched in the mind of Herod, it was hatched in "the boardroom of satan." It was his first attempt to take out the Savior of the world.

But I'm going to suggest a new thought *(to me)*. Satan had to know that the Messiah had come to pay humanity's sin penalty and that it meant that Messiah **was going to die!** Few humans seemed to catch on, but Isaiah 53 *(700 years before)* had made it abundantly clear that the coming Messiah would be a "suffering Savior." "His life would be made an offering for sin." *(Isaiah 53:10)*

- The prophet Daniel *(600 years before)* had made it abundantly clear *(in Daniel 9:25)* that the "Messaic Nagad" the "Messiah Prince" would arrive 483 years after the King of Persia announced the rebuilding of Jerusalem's walls; And the Messiah Prince did arrive, right on time, on Palm Sunday 483 *(lunar)* years later. That's why thousands ran to meet the man on a donkey shouting, "Blessed is he who comes in the name of the Lord!" They had been watching their calendars!

- But in the very next verse Daniel had prophesied that <u>the Messiah Prince would then be killed</u>!

Daniel 9:26: "After this period of sixty-two sets of seven, the Anointed One will be killed, appearing to have accomplished nothing, and a ruler will arise whose armies will destroy the city and the Temple." *(That's exactly what happened with General Titus in 70 A.D.!)*

Satan and his minions had been hearing these verses read for centuries. So when they convinced Herod to kill the babies, they must have believed that they could take Jesus out before he accomplished his mission.

Even when they brought him to death on a cross, in their warped sin-crazed thinking, they thought they were killing him before he could pay the sin debt of the world! They missed the fact that their ignorant actions… <u>are what **caused** him to pay the sin debt of the world</u>!

- But are we getting some sense of the magnitude of the battle that was going on beneath the surface during Jesus' ministry!
- Some 6,000 demons are terrorized by the very sight of Jesus.
- But at the exact same time, other fearful demons are building hatred into the Pharisees, and convincing some of the thousands of people that Jesus had healed to stand outside the mockery of a trial and yell, "Crucify him – crucify him!"
- And they're building into Pontius Pilate a gutlessness that would allow him to let the Pharisees conduct such a trial that was not even legal.

It was a cosmic war!
It still is!

Again, let's ask ourselves this question: In this task of being soldiers in the Lord's army, are we supposed to be "defensive soldiers" just trying to hold the fort against a strong and vicious enemy, or are we supposed to be "offensive soldiers" where we pick up the "Sword of the Spirit" and start doing some damaging, eternal slicing and dicing?

Somehow, God needs to change the picture in the minds of (we) his Church – from us cowering in front of satan, to seeing satan cowering in front of our Savior!

I'm not even beginning to suggest that we arrogantly take on satan in our own strength. Some of us may want to swing the pendulum too far in the "I'll smack satan in the nose" direction.

- But you just as certainly have to understand that **you are one of God's Redeemed children! You are one of God's Blood-Washed Saints!**

- **That changes absolutely everything in your relationship to God, and everything in your relationship with satan and his minions!** *(minion: an underling)*

Your Savior is the one who loved you so much that he died for your sins. He's the One who loves you so much that he sent his own Holy Spirit to indwell you, to transform you from the inside out. He's the same One who so loves you, that he longs to spend all of eternity with you communing in his presence. **That Savior's very presence brings the minions of satan, onto their slimy, evil faces quivering in terror!** *(We'll talk more about why in the next chapter.)*

- Please keep these truths hammering into the front of your mind. The idea that we can personally take on satan in our own power is foolish and dangerous.

- But the idea that you, as a Redeemed child of God, have to be cowering in terror before satan <u>when the Spirit of the Incarnate Son of God dwells within you, filling you, and empowering you</u> – is utter nonsense!

*The same "Spirit of God who raised
Jesus from the dead lives in you!"
(Romans 8:11)*

You are an "in-his-image" Son or Daughter of the Creator of the Universe! Your adversary satan is going to spend all of eternity in the lake of fire! You are going to spend all of eternity in Heaven in the presence of your loving Savior!

The same Jesus, who had 6,000 demons quivering in fear, submitted to death – he died and rose again not only to save you from sin, but also to save you from satan! It is Jesus' power within you that allows you to resist the devil and he will be forced to flee from you! *(James 4:7)*

———————————————

Let's start to put what we are reading into a verbal theology. Please read this slowly, one phrase at a time:

1) "I am strong in the Lord and in his mighty power." I am an over-comer! I am a Christian soldier – called out, in-filled, empowered, and deployed as one of God's spiritual warriors!

2) I start from a position of victory because my Divine Commander has already fought and won ahead of me. I have been commissioned by Jesus to enforce the victory he already won on the cross! I am guaranteed to be a conqueror. "I am MORE than a conqueror!"

3) "I am not fighting against flesh-and-blood enemies, but against mighty powers in this dark world, and against evil spirits in heavenly places. <u>I am able to stand firm against all strategies of the devil</u>!"

4) "My weapons are not human weapons - My 'weapons' have Divine power to demolish satan's strongholds." My "weapon of choice" is PRAYER! My prayers have the authority to turn the tide of evil back from my family, my church, my community, my nation, and my world!

Chapter 3

"Why are you interfering with me, Jesus, Son of the Most, High God? Please, I beg you, don't torture me!"

Let's jump right back into the story of "the most demon-possessed man" in all of Scripture and fill in some more details beyond what we saw in the last chapter. We'll review and then we'll shift up a couple of gears.

1) We are supposed to notice in this account that this poor man's demon spokesman said the demons in him were **Legion**. In the first century that usually meant the number 6,000. We find 15 other people in the New Testament that are demon possessed, and most of the time just one demon ruins their lives. This man has somehow acquired 6,000 evil "possessors" who are in total control of his soul, body and mind.

2) We are supposed to notice that this man ran around naked, blood running from open wounds where he constantly slashed himself with stones. He was a constant threat to the surrounding villagers. The villagers had tried to arrest him, but he would snap the chains and run back to live in the tombs with dead people!

3) We are supposed to notice that when Jesus and his disciples unexpectedly land their boat at the base of "his" mountain pockmarked with tomb openings. The man, predictably, ran toward them with the demons in him, letting out their combined blood curdling screams. This boatful of victims had foolishly placed themselves between the mountain and the water with no chance of getting away from the murderous wrath of 6,000 human-hating demons!

And then <u>something amazing happened</u>!

Let's back up a little bit and fill in some more details:

Luke 8:22: "One day Jesus said to his disciples, 'Let's cross to the other side of the lake.'"

Luke 8:26: "So they arrived in the region of the Gerasenes (*Gadarenes*), **across the lake from Galilee."**

What those two sentences don't include is the fact that they had boarded the boat as hundreds of people were crushing up against Jesus, because he had been graciously healing so many sick people. As he is pinned up against the sea, some sharp dude (*maybe Peter or John*) must have pulled their boat against the shore and said, **"Jump in Jesus!"** And Jesus and his disciples piled in.

What those two sentences don't include is that once they got out into the middle of the 13 mile long lake, a huge storm swept in over the mountains (*probably from the Galilee side of the sea*) and drove the boat to the southeast side of the lake. It was a pagan place where they would not normally have landed, precisely because of what we are getting ready to see happen.

What these two sentences don't tell us is that as the boat was about to sink, Jesus calms the massive storm and the astounded, exhausted soaked-to-the-skin disciples beach their boat to drain out the water. But they are without question uneasy.

- They had landed directly at the base of a pagan graveyard where lots of people had been buried.
- Nobody was being buried there anymore because *(as Matthew records)* at least two demon-possessed men were living in the tombs with the skeletons, terrorizing everyone who came near.
- **And "Mr. Legion" had an all-time world record for the most demons living in any one person.** What could he have possibly done in his life for that to happen? It's hard to imagine!

Luke 8:27-28: "As Jesus was climbing out of the boat, a man who was possessed by demons came out to meet him. For a long time he had been homeless and naked, living in the tombs outside the town. As soon as he saw Jesus, he shrieked and fell down in front of him."

Don't miss the importance of what is happening! This is a man no humans would go near. When they gathered their local SWAT team to take him down, the entire team wrestled him to the ground and wrapped every strong chain around him they could find:

Luke 8:29: "Even when he was placed under guard and put in chains and shackles, he simply broke them and rushed out into the wilderness, completely under the demon's power."

I told you in the last chapter about the demon-possessed man who I watched delivered from a demon as a boy. The people in my church didn't just ask the man to be seated. It took several of the biggest men in our church to wrestle him to the ground as he was making his way toward the Pastor with strange noises coming out of his mouth. That presumably was one demon – this guy had a whole legion!

Luke 8:28: "As soon as he saw Jesus, he shrieked and fell down in front of him." *(We so need this picture to lodge in each one of our minds!)*

The demons who utterly controlled the man, *(he was completely powerless)* and had been terrorizing the whole region of pagan Gadara – **those demons were shrieking and falling down when they saw Jesus!**

Δεκάπολις- Decapolis
Deca- 10 ; polis- city

When I say "pagan" region, don't imagine a few stone huts. The massive stone theater in this picture was already there when Jesus walked this earth. He probably saw it, or sat in it! If we are not watching closely we might miss that the end of Mark 7 connects to Mark 8 – and we may not realize that the events of Mark 8, including the feeding of the 4,000, also will take place in "the Decapolis."

The city you see in the background of the picture is modern day Amman, Jordan. *(And there are lots of other ruins in the region.)* The Romans had come in and re-built ten impressive cities and the whole 10-city region was called – the Decapolis.

But as impressive as the cities were, their religions were still Greek and Roman paganism. That always included the worship of idols, the offering of human sacrifices to those idols, and the use of slave temple prostitutes involving the perverse abuse of the most innocent in their society. But the whole region of those godless, sinful, child-sacrificing people found demonic Mr. Legion way too far into the blackness for even them to deal with!

Then that horrible satan-filled human being meets Jesus!

Luke 8:28: "As soon as he saw Jesus, he shrieked and fell down in front of him. Then he screamed, 'Why are you interfering with me, Jesus, Son of the Most, High God? Please, I beg you, don't torture me!'"

Say it with me: "What I see and hear when demons meet Jesus and scream out in terror in Scripture should make me never live in fear of them again in my life **because the actual truth is <u>demons are scared to death of my God</u>!**"

"They are scared out of their minds of my Savior!!"
Is that sentence ringing in your soul?

- Your Savior, the One who declared and still declares He loves you so much that he would allow himself to be crucified to pay the penalty for your sins.
- The One who loves you so much that after dying and then rising from the dead to forgive you and cleanse you, he would then send his own Holy Spirit to indwell you – to transform you from the inside out!
- That One who loves you so much that he longs to spend all of eternity communing with you.

That Savior's very presence caused the minions of satan to quiver in terror – <u>every single time</u>!

And here's why! Listen to the tortured screams coming out of the demoniac:

Luke 8:28: "As soon as he saw Jesus, he shrieked and fell down in front of him. Then he screamed, 'Why are you interfering with me, Jesus, Son of the Most, High God? Please, I beg you, don't torture me!'"

- There are people sitting in churches all over the world who *(even though they are occupying a church seat)* will deny that Jesus is divine!
- They will swear *(on a stack of Bibles)* that Jesus was just a good man with some particularly wise things to say

about loving everybody, being tolerant of everybody, and treating others the way you want to be treated.

- "But let's not go all nuts," they will say, "and make Jesus out to be incarnate God, here on earth in a human body."

In direct contrast, these <u>demons clearly believed Jesus was Sovereign</u>! They believed, without question, that he had complete authority and that authority extended over them!

So, for those who don't believe the Bible means exactly what it seems to be saying, I can assure you that satan and his demons do!

Even the demon's "End-Times view" thoroughly assumes a returning Christ and a coming judgment over sin and satan. Watch this:

Matthew 8:29: "'What do you want with us, Son of God?' they shouted. 'Have you come here to torture us <u>before the appointed time</u>?'"

Luke 8:31: "And they begged Jesus repeatedly <u>not to order them to go into the Abyss</u>."

Again, what "theology" are these God-hating demons pointing to that eventually arrives through the pen of the Apostle John in inspired Scripture?

Revelation 20:1-2,10: "And I saw an angel coming down out of heaven, having the key to the Abyss and holding in his hand a great chain. He seized the dragon, that ancient serpent, <u>who is the devil, or Satan</u>, and bound

him for a thousand years." *(Revelation 20:10 then says satan gets out briefly to gather those who still reject Jesus during the 1000-year Millenium.)* **"And the devil, who deceived them, was thrown into the lake of burning sulfur, where the beast and the false prophet had been thrown. They will be tormented day and night for ever and ever."**

Based on what the demons are saying, they already know that they will also be in the lake of fire with satan forever. Notice, the demons believe their total destruction is still a "future event." They obviously believe Revelation 20 more firmly than many Christians do!

Demons apparently know, and believe, that the Bible says Jesus' coming would bring an "eternal kingdom" which would forever wipe out their kingdom. *But they had the same problem as the first century Jews:* **They didn't understand that Jesus was going to come twice!**

In Jesus' First Coming he would pay our sin debt, but in His Second Coming he would set up an Everlasting Kingdom, and all the Redeemed Saints *(us)* will forever reign with Him!

The point is; the evil one, the one we often see as an almost insurmountable adversary,

- ✓ one single word from our Savior's mouth,
- ✓ the same Savior who satan knows that John 1 says was the Creator of the Universe,

- ✓ the same Savior who one of these days is going to become the Sovereign Judge of the Universe!
- ✓ One word from that Savior's mouth, and our "powerful" adversary turns into a quivering ball of terror! *Again:*

God needs to change the picture in the minds of his Church, from us cowering in front of satan, to seeing satan cowering in front of our Savior!

But, but Sam,

1 Peter 5:8 describes satan as a "roaring lion" prowling around seeking who he may devour.

Psalm 100:3 says: "<u>We are his people, the sheep of his pasture</u>."

See there, we learned that in Sunday School! Satan is the "roaring lion" looking to devour me! I'm just one of Jesus' helpless sheep praying that my shepherd, Jesus, can protect me from the big bad lion. *(The Greek word for that theology in the New Testament is; "Baloney!" – pronounced buh-low-nee.)*

Maybe it's way past time to change our mental snapshot!

At the very least **we need to see ourselves as "<u>Warrior Sheep</u>!"**

But more accurately we need to see ourselves as **Christian Soldiers – Spiritual Warriors!**

- We're called by God to fight off the powers of darkness in our lives, our family's lives, our community, our state, our nation, our world!
- We sometimes get all caught up in how being a newly converted Christian remakes the sinner into a "baby Christian."
- But is being "born again" just another way of saying we're re-born as innocent, helpless, incapable-of-caring-for-ourselves babies?

Helpless is what happens when we are physically born of human parents. Being "born again," or **being "born of the Spirit" leaves one empowered – not helpless**!

When we are "born again" we are not dropped into a human maternity ward, but into a **cosmic war zone!** You get to take your "first steps" in the middle of a worldwide spiritual battle for the eternal souls of humanity, including your own!

Ephesians 6:12: "For we are not fighting against flesh-and-blood enemies, but against evil rulers and authorities of the unseen world, against mighty powers in this dark world, and against evil spirits in the heavenly places." Yes? Yes!

2 Corinthians 10:3-4: "For though we live in the world, we do not wage war as the world does. The weapons we fight with are not the weapons of the

world. On the contrary, they have divine power to demolish strongholds!" Amen? Amen!

Let's get back to the amazing Luke 8 account. We're supposed to feel the suspense as the demons wait in terror for Jesus' decision. <u>Will he, or will he not, send them into the bottomless abyss "before their time"</u>?

- Question: If they are going to be in the Abyss for all eternity, what does it matter when their sentence begins? Here's why: Because satan and his minions remain convinced that they are going to find a way to thwart their eternal destiny!

- Right at that very moment, satan was working out a plan that would cause the Pharisees and religious leaders to sentence the Messiah Savior to death. If only they could destroy him before he eternally punished them! *(They thought!)*

- Surely satan had to know better! He was with God before the fall probably as an archangel. He has to understand God's infinite power, doesn't he?

- He did. *(He had.)* But the result of God's presence leaving satan completely was to **leave him "irrationally illogical**." Satan is now a liar. He is the father of lies. He lies all the time. He can't not lie! He can't even think in terms of the truth. **He continuously lies, <u>even to himself</u>!**

- Notice this: when you see sin-bound people making the most ridiculously, illogical decisions, it is because they are being led by a master who has lost all touch with what truth even is!

So Legion's spokesman has what the demons thought was a good suggestion:

> **Mark 5:11-13: "There happened to be a large herd of pigs feeding on the hillside nearby. 'Send us into those pigs,' the spirits begged. 'Let us enter them. ' So Jesus gave them permission. The evil spirits came out of the man and entered the pigs, and the entire herd of about 2,000 pigs plunged down the steep hillside into the lake and drowned in the water."**

I told you, in the last chapter, that this was the first known incidence of "deviled ham"! That's not my joke. It's been around for a long time. This one has too: The pigs all ran down the cliff and did a "swine-dive" into the water. *Funny!* *– but:*

- We see the demons begging Jesus – begging him not to send them into the abyss, begging to be allowed to go into the pigs.

- Demons seem to always want to function inside of some living thing. Remember when Jesus talked about demons who were cast out and how they would wander around trying to find a new home? *(Luke 11: 24-26)*

- Notice this: These demons had to ask Jesus' permission before they could do anything! It's important to notice the demons were and are totally under Jesus' control!

So, Jesus said, "OK, you can go into the pigs!" Why did he do that? I actually think the answer might be very simple. Jesus has to be able to show that the demons had left the man. That was how he was going to display his divine power! If all 2,000 pigs were affected, it would be sudden and vivid proof that his power had complete control over the demons. It would also show everybody just how serious the man's possession had actually been. It would also expose the deadly intentions of the demons. Demons kill! Demons destroy!

- The demons begged for a new home in the pigs, but their pure evil power immediately overwhelmed and killed the pigs!

- People sometimes ask: "Why would Jesus kill all those pigs?" He didn't, the demons did!

 Pigs can swim quite well. *(You can go on YouTube and watch swimming pigs all day long.)*

Pigs are very tough animals. They could take a "swine dive" off a cliff, hit the water, and keep right on swimming, but obviously not when their every action is controlled by evil demons.

I used to take "defensive driving classes" every year so I could drive an ambulance. They taught us: "never hit a pig." A pig can flip your vehicle upside down in an instant.

And then we had a family in our church who did hit a pig, and it did serious damage to them and their vehicle.

Pigs are tough!

But these particular pigs became maniac pigs just like the man had been, and the maniac man became perfectly normal once he met Jesus!

> **Luke 8:34-36: "When the herdsmen saw it, they fled to the nearby town and the surrounding countryside, spreading the news as they ran. People rushed out to see what had happened. A crowd soon gathered around Jesus, and they saw the man who had been freed from the demons. He was sitting at Jesus' feet, fully clothed and perfectly <u>sane</u>, and they were all afraid. Then those who had seen what happened told the others how the demon-possessed man had been healed."**

- Sane: the word used is **"sophroneo" – thinking with wisdom**. It was a visible radical change from a mental maniac.

  1) Instead of being naked, he's wearing clothes.

  2) Instead of running back to the dead in the tombs, he's sitting in front of the Creator of all Life.

3) It is a picture of complete transformation! The phrase "made well" comes from the Greek word "sozo." There was undoubtedly some conversation between the man and Jesus that we don't have because **the man had not only been saved from the power of satan, he had been saved from the power of sin!**

Mark's account said this whole thing was such a big deal, that "everybody" in the whole region came rushing out to see the transformed man. Everybody had been so terrorized by what was obviously the "evilest of the evil."

Surely everybody is going to be so happy with the rabbi that has delivered them from the terrorism that had plagued them! Right? They will surely pour out their thanks to Jesus. They will surely invite him to their towns to see who else can be transformed – Yes? They will undoubtedly give him the keys to the city, all ten cities for that matter! Right? Nope!

> **Luke 8:37: "And <u>all the people</u> in the region of the Gerasenes begged Jesus to go away and leave them alone, for a great wave of fear swept over them."**

- Well, they are probably just upset over the loss of the pigs? Yes? No! There is no further mention of the pigs or their owners. Nobody seems to care!
- The fact that the owner had the pigs grazing right where nobody else in the region would ever go might tell us something!

But these "Decapolis" people were terrified! They knew exactly what had happened because three Gospels say that "everybody discussed every detail." But **they ended up more terrified of the man who healed the demoniac than they were of the evil demoniac himself!**

On the other side of the lake people had crammed against the boat not wanting Jesus to leave. On this side of the lake people are crammed against the boat saying "get out of here! We don't want your kind on this side of the sea." Jesus' righteousness had so exposed their own sinfulness, that rather than being willing to confess it and be transformed and saved, they wanted the Transformer Savior gone!

- Do you ever wish God would do bigger, more obvious miracles in our own day? If only he would, sinners would certainly drop their sinfulness and come running to Jesus' salvation? Right? Not according to these examples!

- Just as Jesus is doing this amazing miracle in Gadara the religious leaders on the other side of the Sea of Galilee, who had all seen him do thousands and thousands of miracles – **are plotting his execution!**

Thankfully, that's not the end of the story!

> **Luke 8:38-39: "The man who had been freed from the demons begged to go with him. But Jesus sent him home, saying, 'No, go back to your family, and tell them every-thing God has done for you.'** *(He clearly didn't stop with his family.)* **"So he went all through the town** (*Mark says "all*

the Decapolis") **proclaiming the great things Jesus had done for him!"**

And my, did the saved demoniac ever have a strong message! "I was the most demon-possessed person on the planet! A storm blew the Jewish Messiah to our shores, and all the demons inside of me shivered in terror at the sight of him! He commanded them, and they left me, and then he forgave my sins, and I am now saved! I am transformed!"

And if he did that for me, he will meet every need in each of your lives as well!

Tradition tells us a large church did rise up in the Decapolis, perhaps initially started by this man's testimony. But notice this:

- After the Mark 5 account – in Mark 7, Jesus purposely walked right back into the Decapolis. He's still there in Mark 8. He heals the deaf man and then people begin to gather around him - there are 4,000 *(probably men with three times that in women and children).* Then the great "feeding of the 4,000" miracle takes place!

- Eusebius, the church historian, records that within forty years the region became almost completely Christian, increased greatly by Christians escaping to that region before the destruction of Jerusalem. *(Eusebius 3.5.3)*

But this book isn't about the missionary part of it. **This book is about the power of God-over-satan part!** I've personalized these six points so they can become your personal statements:

1) The same Jesus who ordered 6,000 demons out of Legion that day is the same Jesus who loved me so much that he died for my sins!

2) The same Jesus, who had 6,000 demons that day quivering in fear, submitted to death on a cross, not only to save me from sin, but to save me from the power of satan!

3) **Romans 8:11: "The <u>Spirit of God, who raised Jesus from the dead, lives in me</u>! And just as God raised Christ Jesus from the dead, he will give life to my mortal body by this same Spirit living within me."**

4) Jesus crushed the power of satan by his death and resurrection **"so that by his death he might break the power of him who holds the power of death, that is the devil, and free those who all their lives were held in slavery by their fear of death."** *(Hebrews 2:14-15)*

5) <u>Satan doesn't have the right to control me anymore</u>! I am a Redeemed Son or Daughter of the Most, High God!

6) I can resist satan and he will flee from me, not because I am strong in myself, but because through the redeeming power of Jesus' death and resurrection – the God who now lives in me, giving life to my mortal body, <u>scares satan out of his mind</u>!

Let's expand our final declaration! Say this out loud as you read it:

"I am strong in the Lord and in his mighty power." I am an over-comer! I am a Christian soldier called out, in-filled, empowered, and deployed as one of God's spiritual warriors!

I start from a position of victory because my Divine Commander has already fought, and won ahead of me. I have been commissioned by Jesus to enforce the victory he already won on the cross! I am guaranteed to be a conqueror... "I am MORE than a conqueror!"

"My weapons are not human weapons - My 'weapons' have Divine power to demolish satan's strongholds." My "weapon of choice" is PRAYER! My prayers have the authority to turn the tide of evil back from my family, my church, my community, my nation, and my world.

"I am not fighting against flesh and blood enemies, but against mighty powers in this dark world, and against evil spirits in heavenly places." But "I am able to stand firm against all strategies of the devil!"

I AM JESUS' CHURCH! "The gates of hell will not prevail against me. I have received the keys of the kingdom of heaven, and whatever I bind on earth has already been bound in heaven!"

I believe that my prayers will release the mighty power of God to accomplish in my family, my church, my community, and my nation what God has already planned in heaven!

All that is needed to unlock the mighty unlimited, resources of heaven is for me to insert the keys I have been given – the keys of powerful, effective, God-filled prayer!

I believe that my prayers will foil the plans of satan and bring his evil strategies to a standstill. "I can resist satan and he will flee from me!"

I WILL pray! I will be victorious! "I am strong in the Lord and in his mighty power. I am more than a conqueror through Christ Jesus who loves me!"

WHAT SCARES DEMONS: Part II

I apologize in advance for the sheer number of exclamation points in the following section.

It is virtually impossible to write on the following truths without jamming your finger down on the exclamation point key!!

Chapter 4

"Whatever you bind on earth has already been bound in heaven."

So satan and his minions did, of course, succeed in killing the Messiah, just as Daniel had prophesied, *(Daniel 9:26)* but it was all a divine set-up! **Jesus planned his own death to pay for our sins**! *(He used satan and his demons like pawns to carry out what he had planned from the beginning!)*

But Jesus didn't stay dead! He defeated death itself and rose victorious from the grave! His resurrection was the ultimate victory because he defeated not only death, but also satan, and sin, and hell, and he opened the door for each of us to experience forgiveness, heart cleansing, and eternal life!

Colossians 2:14-15: "He (Jesus) **canceled the record of the charges against us and took it away by nailing it to the cross. In this way, he disarmed** *(stripped the power and weapons from)* **the spiritual rulers and authorities** *(satan and his demons).* **He shamed them publicly by his victory over them on the cross.** *(He made a public spectacle of them, triumphing over them by the cross.)"*

- Jesus stripped satan of any legitimate claim over our lives! He defanged the "roaring lion." He ripped the "dominion of the earth" away from satan!

- The same Jesus, who had Mr. Legion's demons quivering in fear, submitted to death on the cross, **not only to save you from sin, but to save you from the power of satan!**

- Satan doesn't have the right to control you anymore! You are a Redeemed Son or Daughter of the Most, High God! **"The Spirit of God, who raised Jesus from the dead, now lives in you!"** *(Romans 8:11)*

Is this truth burying itself in your soul?

———————————

OK Chess, that's all well and good, but now what?

If Jesus destroyed the works of satan on the cross and completely defeated the evil-one through his resurrection from the dead, **why is the devil still here?** And why do I seem to find myself in a battle with him every day of my life?

> **1 John 5:18-19: "We know that God's children do not make a practice of sinning, for <u>God's Son holds them securely</u>, <u>and the evil one cannot touch them</u>. We know that we are children of God and that the world around us is under the control of the evil one."**

So did God's plan backfire? Was Jesus' "defeat" of satan not big enough? Did Jesus' death and resurrection provide for

72

my "afterlife" but fail to address the raging spiritual needs in my present life?

If God is planning to exile satan and his demons into the lake of fire, <u>why didn't he just do it the day after he rose from the grave</u>?

Clearly God's unfolding plan of redemption was not completely finished with Jesus' resurrection!

- The power of satan to control the human heart was broken. Salvation was provided for all who believe.

- But there was still the need for Jesus' disciples to take the Good News to the whole world, 99.99% of which were still pagan. *(Matthew 24:14)*

- There was still the promised "coming and infilling" of the Holy Spirit's presence who would empower Jesus' followers and transform them from the inside out. They would be radically changed from followers of satan to followers of God, from the kingdom of darkness to the kingdom of Light! *(John 16:13-14, Colossians 1:13)*

I WILL BUILD MY CHURCH
and the gates of hell will not overpower it

There was still the birth and growth of the Church that **Jesus declared he was going to build, and the gates of hell would not be able to prevail against it!** *(Matthew 16:18)*

73

"Whatever the church would bind on earth would have already been bound (ἔσται δεδεμένον, *It's a perfect passive participle)* **in heaven, and whatever the church would loose on earth would have been already loosed** (ἔσται λελυμένον) **in heaven."** *(Matthew 16:19)*

Jesus had defeated the forces of sin and satan on the cross. He broke the power of satan. He provided freedom from sin to those "who all their lives were held in slavery by their fear of death."

All of that did happen! Scripture is very clear. But it is also very clear in telling us that the whole overarching plan of redemption was not yet complete (*is* not yet complete!).

- This Church Jesus said he was going to build,
- He didn't say the gates of hell would not come against it,
- He said the gates of hell would not prevail against it!
- The Church would be able to overcome the gates of hell/hades! *(Binding and loosing on earth as in heaven!)*

So, if Jesus was going to plant this Church, this growing group of Redeemed People stretching out to every remote part of the earth – and at the same time Jesus planned to leave satan and his minions on this planet, there was bound to be some serious conflict!

There was going to be a spiritual war! His followers, for however many years were going to tick by before Jesus' Second Coming, were going to have to learn to battle and defeat satan, just like their Savior had battled and defeated satan!

- This wasn't a failure of the original plan. This wasn't a plan B to correct the original plan A. **This was plan A!**

- This was all part of the Redemption that God had fully planned out, before the foundations of the world! *(Revelation 13:8)*

Jesus had fully defeated satan, breaking the chains he had on human souls! But now thousands, then millions, of his beloved Redeemed were going to have to learn to battle the evil one and win!

Why? What was the point? What could possibly be the purpose of leaving satan here as Jesus' church is born, and then grows across the planet?

What was to be the end result of the Redeemed Saints learning to battle and defeat satan and his minions? If the Church is supposed to be binding and loosing on earth what has already been bound and loosed in heaven, might this be exactly what/who they are supposed to be binding and loosing? What in the world is God up to?

Clearly the Bible paints Christians as being locked in a spiritual battle. Most of us can look at our lives this last week and see the spiritual war raging in our personal lives, our families, our community, our country, and our world. You simply can't miss it! And while we've already said:

- Satan doesn't have the right to control you anymore! You are a Redeemed Son or Daughter of the Most, High God!

- That sure doesn't mean satan is not going to try! And "the Spirit of God, who raised Jesus from the dead now living in you" – is precisely how you are going to defeat every advance of the evil one!

Ephesians 6:12: "For we are not fighting against flesh-and-blood enemies, but against evil rulers and authorities of the unseen world, against mighty powers in this dark world, and against evil spirits in the heavenly places."

2 Corinthians 10:3-4: "For though we live in the world, we do not wage war as the world does. The weapons we fight with are not the weapons of the world. On the contrary, they have divine power to demolish strongholds."

Clearly Jesus had/has no intentions of us losing the battle against satan! He has provided the saving grace, the training of his Word, the infilling empowering Holy Spirit, and every spiritual weapon we need to fight the battle and win so that the gates of hell will not prevail against us!

Romans 8:35, 37: "Can anything ever separate us from Christ's love? Does it mean he no longer loves us if we have trouble or calamity, or are persecuted, or hungry, or destitute, or in danger, or threatened with death? No, despite all these things, OVERWHELMING VICTORY IS OURS *(we are more than conquerors)* through Christ, who loves us."

Romans 8:38-39: "And I am convinced that nothing can ever separate us from God's love. Neither death nor life, NEITHER ANGELS NOR DEMONS, neither our fears for today nor our worries about tomorrow—NOT EVEN THE POWERS OF HELL can separate us from God's love. No power in the sky above or in the earth below—indeed, nothing in all creation will ever be able to separate us from the love of God that is revealed in Christ Jesus our Lord."

Overwhelming victory is ours – over what, over whom? When you get to heaven and "Saint Peter asks at the Pearly Gates," ☺ "Were you victorious, during your brief stay on earth," What is he going to be talking about?

- Will he mean did you conquer your educational pursuits and end up at the top of your field? Everybody knows that the highest educated people here on earth will have the highest positions in heaven, right?

- Isn't it true that those who achieve the greatest visible success here on earth will be the most rewarded in heaven?

- **No!** All of our guts tell us that there will be uneducated, invisible, seeming nobody's here on earth who will be honored far above many, many others in heaven! Yes?

  Revelation 3:20-21: "Look! I stand at the door and knock. If you hear my voice and open the door, I will come in, and we will share a meal together as friends. <u>Those who are victorious</u>" *(him/her who overcomes).*

Victorious over who? What are we supposed to be overcoming?

When your stay on earth is analyzed and the box is checked, She was an Overcomer! He was an Overcomer! What will that mean? There is a clue here in verse 21.

We often pull verse 20 and use it alone. Did you ever notice which of the seven churches verse 20 was written to? <u>Laodicea</u>, the lukewarm church!

Jesus is saying, "Out with lukewarm Christianity! I'm knocking at your lukewarm heart's door. Open the door to real fellowship with me, and I'll achieve in you the reason I put you on this planet!"   But watch what Jesus' Revelation says next:

> **Revelation 3:20-21: "Look! I stand at the door and knock. If you hear my voice and open the door, I will come in and we will share a meal (*fellowship*) together as friends. <u>Those who are victorious, (*overcome*) will sit with me on my throne, just as I was victorious (overcame) and sat with my Father on his throne</u>."** *(Did you see that?)*

Our "victorious overcoming" on this earth is supposed to be the same kind of "victorious overcoming" Jesus experienced when he was here!

Clearly it had/has little to do with education or vocation. Jesus' victorious overcoming has everything to do with what we've been discussing in this book!

1) As we said, God gave Adam and Eve rulership/dominion over the earth.

2) When Adam and Eve transferred their allegiance to satan, they transferred the "dominion" of the earth. *(That's why the Epistles call satan "the god of this world, the prince of the power of the air.")* But watch this huge change:

3) When Jesus died to redeem us and rose from the dead to offer us eternal life, forgiveness from and victory over sin that was all made possible because the <u>authority, dominion, and/or rulership had been regained</u> by Jesus' triumph over satan! Jesus then declared "all authority in heaven and earth has been given to him"! *What must all of that mean?*

Let me enlarge the context of the Colossians 2 passage:

Colossians 2:12-15: "You were raised to new life because you trusted the mighty power of God, who raised Christ from the dead. You were dead because of your sins and because your sinful nature was not yet cut away. Then God made you alive with Christ, for he forgave all our sins. He canceled the record of the charges against us and took it away by nailing it to the cross. In this way, he <u>(*Jesus*) disarmed the spiritual rulers and authorities</u>. He shamed them publicly by his victory over them on the cross."

- God ripped the dominion of the earth away from satan. <u>So who then ended up with the long lost dominion</u>? It was given to Adam and Eve by God. Adam and Eve transferred it to satan. Jesus ripped it away from satan by his victory on the cross and over death. **So, who has the dominion over all of creation now?**

Matthew 28:18-20: "Jesus came and told his disciples, '<u>I have been given ALL AUTHORITY IN HEAVEN AND ON EARTH.</u>' *Then he added:*

'Therefore, go and make disciples of all the nations… And be sure of this: <u>I am with you always, even to the end of the age.</u>'" *With us, for what? – To do what?*

- Do we get the significance of the <u>All authority is given to Jesus</u> part of that?
- When we look at the sinful world around us – do we think in terms of Jesus having ALL AUTHORITY?
- What is the significance of Jesus linking the "all authority has been given to me" with the next phrase: "I am with you always, even to the end of the age"?

Let me quote what I wrote in **Unmasking Revelation** *(pg. 151)*

Jesus broke the stranglehold satan held on the hearts of mankind! That is not the same thing as saying that Jesus "took charge of the earth" reducing satan to utter impotence. **That has not happened yet, <u>but it will</u>!**

When, when will it happen? When will Jesus take complete charge? <u>When will "the kingdoms of this world become the kingdoms of our Lord, and of His Christ"</u>?

Revelation 11:15-17: "The *seventh angel sounded his trumpet*, and there were loud voices in heaven, which said: <u>'The kingdom of the world has become the kingdom of our Lord and of his Messiah, and He will reign for ever and ever.</u>' And the twenty-four elders, who were seated on their thrones before God, fell on their faces and worshiped God, saying: 'We give thanks to you, Lord God Almighty,

the One who is and who was, because <u>you have taken your great power and have begun to reign</u>.'"

- Clearly there is a space of time between when Jesus defeats satan, when all authority on heaven and earth is given to him – and when Jesus finally says: "That's enough!" And he takes the total reins of the earth and begins to pour out his judgment on sin and satan.
- Revelation lays that out clearly at the time of the Rapture – *(IMO)*. At the end of Revelation 6 and the beginning of Revelation 7, "the End of the Age" is described.
- Then comes this powerful statement in chapter 11 about Jesus finally taking complete power over the earth and beginning his everlasting reign!
- The period in between Jesus defeating satan, and him finally taking over the complete reigns of this earth and setting up his everlasting rule **is the Church Age. Right now! We are living in it!**

So, what are we supposed to be doing? If the "overcoming" of Jesus on this earth has to do with him taking on the evil one and winning, what is "**<u>our victorious overcoming</u>**" supposed to be?

If Jesus' victory over satan led to him sitting with his Father on His throne, is our "victorious overcoming" supposed to lead to us sitting with Jesus on His throne?

(I'm not making up words here!)

Revelation 3:21: "Those who are victorious, (*overcome*) will sit with me on my throne, just as I was victorious (*overcame*) and sat with my Father on his throne!"

This is some kind of heavy theology, isn't it? It's one thing to talk about confessing our sins, having them forgiven, and being assured of a place in heaven.

It seems a lot more difficult to talk about us, using this life to learn to overcome the evil one, and **us learning to overcome satan as somehow the "training ground" for us reigning with Christ** in all of eternity!

It sounds almost weird doesn't it – mystical? But it is actually exactly what the Bible is saying. We're just a little scared to talk about it because it has such huge implications!

2 Timothy 2:8, 10-12: "Remember Jesus Christ, raised from the dead... Therefore I endure everything for the sake of the elect, that they too may obtain the salvation that is in Christ Jesus... Here is a trustworthy saying: If we died with him, we will also live with him; <u>if we endure, we will also reign with him</u>." *Endure what? What are we standing up against in this life?*

This is a whole lot more than "I've got a mansion over the hilltop," or "by and by, I'll walk those streets of gold." Who in the world is going to care about gold? (*As many have often noted, in heaven, gold is just pavement!*)

1) Somehow the function of Jesus on this earth in defeating satan and pushing back the powers of darkness has been <u>passed on to you, the Redeemed, the Church!</u>

2) This has become the "training ground" for reigning with Christ in heaven.

3) We have become the "enforcers" of the victory Jesus won on the cross.

4) Jesus could have taken satan completely out, but he didn't! Satan is still here so that you, the Bride of Christ, the Body of Christ, can learn to win over the evil one!

Paul Billheimer wrote a book, *"Destined to Overcome,"* almost 40 years ago. It deeply impacted my young ministry life. He said our God-given tool for enforcing victory over the evil one is the tool of prayer. Effective prayer is the pathway by which we mere humans learn to take on and defeat satan and the forces of darkness. <u>We are the enforcers of the victory Jesus already won</u>!

I would suggest the following "overcoming" theology:

#1) Our "victorious overcoming" on this earth is supposed to be the same kind of "victorious overcoming" Jesus experienced when he was here. The end result will be "reigning with Christ" in heaven.

- I'm not talking about some kind of vague theology here. I'm talking about <u>your present and your eternal future!</u> **YOU!** If you are going to reign with Christ in eternity, it will be because you "overcame" while you were on this earth.

#2) What was the great victory Jesus accomplished here on this earth? *(The "overcoming" victory?)*

- Defeating the power and plan of satan who had all of humanity in his evil grasp.

- Providing forgiveness, redemption, transformation to all who will embrace it.
- Empowering each of those "Believers" to become the mouths and hands and feet to push back against the forces of darkness and to take this message of freedom from sin, and satan, to the ends of the earth!

So is that what our "victorious overcoming" is supposed to look like? Do we cower in the corner hoping that satan, "that roaring lion who is seeking whom he may devour," doesn't find us? Does our victory only consist of deflecting enough of the devil's attacks to slide into heaven bloody and bleeding but still intact. Victory consists of not getting eaten! Yes? No!

It helps me to remember what I was taught when still a young Christian teenager. Young, strong, powerful lions don't roar when they are pursuing their prey. They quietly stalk it and eat it!

It's the old toothless lions, whose power is diminished, who are reduced to roaring at their prey trying to scare it into submission!

So what should my "victorious overcoming" look like?

a) Will I cower, my shield up, hoping to just deflect satan's fiery darts?

OR

b) Will I become a warrior, a Christian Soldier, enforcing the victory Jesus already won on the Cross!

Let's add some more points to our "overcomer" theology: Could it really be that: *(As Paul Billheimer used to teach)*

#3) God entrusted to those who, in the centuries to come, would embrace his gift of salvation the task of enforcing Jesus' victory over sin and satan – *but it goes even further.*

#4) It's through the process of learning to enforce God's will on this earth *(binding and loosing on earth what has already been bound and loosed in heaven),* that we go through the "apprenticeship of learning to reign with Christ" in heaven.

#5) When God delegates to us the authority to become the 'administrators' of carrying out His decisions on this earth – when we effectively do that, we are "receiving on-the-job training for heaven!" *(Could it possibly be so?)*

Let's finish this chapter by yelling out our 'overcoming declaration' one more time:

"I am strong in the Lord and in his mighty power." I am an over-comer! I am a Christian soldier called out, in-filled, empowered, and deployed as one of God's spiritual warriors!

I start from a position of victory because my Divine Commander has already fought and won ahead of me. I have been commissioned by Jesus to enforce the victory he already won on the cross! I am guaranteed to be a conqueror... "I am MORE than a conqueror!"

"My weapons are not human weapons - My 'weapons' have Divine power to demolish satan's strongholds." My "weapon of choice" is PRAYER! My prayers have the authority to turn the tide of evil back from my family, my church, my community, my nation, and my world.

"I am not fighting against flesh and blood enemies, but against mighty powers in this dark world, and against evil spirits in heavenly places." But "I am able to stand firm against all strategies of the devil!"

I AM JESUS' CHURCH! "The gates of hell will not prevail against me. I have received the keys of the kingdom of heaven, and whatever I bind on earth has already been bound in heaven!"

I believe that my prayers will release the mighty power of God to accomplish in my family, my church, my community, and my nation what God has already planned in heaven!

All that is needed to unlock the mighty unlimited, resources of heaven is for me to insert the keys I have been given – the keys of powerful, effective, God-filled prayer!

I believe that my prayers will foil the plans of satan and bring his evil strategies to a standstill. "I can resist satan and he will flee from me!"

I WILL pray! I will be victorious! "I am strong in the Lord and in his mighty power. I am more than a conqueror through Christ Jesus who loves me!"

Chapter 5

"Despite all these things – overwhelming victory is ours!"

We won't go back over ground we have already plowed, but we may need to break the ground up a little bit finer. Let me offer two adjusted statements to begin this chapter:

> You say you have faith, for you believe that there is one God. Good for you! Even the demons believe this, and they tremble in terror.
>
> James 2:19 NLT

Every time Jesus personally came in contact with demons in Scripture they were scared out of their minds, scared of his infinite power over them, scared of the fact that he said he had "prepared an eternal fire for the devil and his angels"! *(Matthew 25:41)*

2) Somehow God wants to change the picture in the minds of his Church – from us cowering defensively in front of satan, to seeing satan cowering defensively in front of our Savior!

So once we established Jesus' complete control over evil, we then turned our attention to what that means to you and me.

- Jesus, after his resurrection, declared that "all power in heaven and on earth had now been given to him."

- He, and then the Epistles, **paint the Followers of Jesus as extensions of the powerful hand of Almighty God**!

- Even as they are being persecuted and martyred the Early Church pushed back against the evil one so hard, that they turned a completely godless pagan world into a burning missionary wall of flame, in just a few generations.

- Far from being powerless in front of an unconquerable evil foe, the New Testament **paints the Believer as a spiritual warrior** who can *(and should)* be conquering evil through the power of Jesus' name and the power of his death and resurrection.

Notice this interesting **"overcomer sandwich"** ☺ that God breathed into Scripture. As soon as the Gospels and Acts are over, even though the history of the birth of Christianity is filled with hardships, including the persecution of the Early Church – God wants to make sure that we all thoroughly understand that what is coming to us, as a result of Jesus' death and resurrection, **is not a life of defeat, but an eternal life of victory!** Something the Apostle Paul calls not just victory, but "overwhelming victory" – not just conquering, but "more than conquering"!

> **Romans 8:37: "No, despite all these things, overwhelming victory is ours (we are more than conquerors) through Christ, who loves us."**

On the other end of what I'm calling "an overcomer sandwich," capping off the end of the Bible in the book of Revelation is this stunning promise that we started looking at in the last chapter. It's so massive that it may be, a little bit, outside our ability to fully understand.

> **Revelation 3:20-21: "Look! (Behold!) I stand at the door and knock. If you hear my voice and open the door, I will come in, and we will fellowship as friends. Those who are victorious, (overcome) will sit with me on my throne, just as I was victorious (overcame) and sat with my Father on his throne."**

Here's an upgraded version of what we concluded at the end of chapter four. See if these points are stirring a spiritual hunger inside of you:

1) Our "victorious overcoming" on this earth is supposed to be the same kind of "victorious overcoming" Jesus experienced when he was here on earth. The end result will be "reigning with Christ" in heaven.

2) And what was the great (overcoming) victory Jesus accomplished here on earth? He defeated the power and plan of satan who had all humanity in his evil grasp! He provided forgiveness, redemption, and transformation to all who would embrace his gift. He empowered all who would "believe" to become his mouth and hands and feet to push back against the forces of darkness! He commissioned them to take his message of freedom from sin, and satan, and death, and hell to the ends of the earth!

3) So what exactly is our commanded "victorious overcoming" supposed to look like? **It's apparently supposed to be the "mirror** *(a human)* **reflection" of what Jesus already accomplished!** *Here's our "mirror image" quiz:*

Q: Has the limited power and evil plan of satan been defeated in my life?

Q: Have I embraced Jesus' forgiveness, heart cleansing, and redemption leading to everlasting life?

Q: Has my "old life" been increasingly transformed by the presence of God through the infilling Holy Spirit?

Q: Have I been empowered as the mouth, hands, and feet of Jesus on this earth, to push back against the forces of darkness? Am I walking that out?

Q: Am I spreading the message of freedom from sin and satan as far as my personal influence can reach?

If you've carefully read every chapter, you may suspect where this trail is leading, but don't rush to get there. We need to logically *(theo-logically)* think through how this very important truth works out in our lives.

1) If the power and plan of satan has been defeated in your life, that would mean that satan's influence is no longer present, right? Apparently not, since each of us have dealt with temptations from satan already today!

2) Has my old sinful life been transformed? YES, yes it has! Many of you can and do testify that you are not even remotely the same sinful person you used to be! *(Maybe some of you can't quite say that – yet.)* But for those who can testify to change, you would probably use a word like <u>transformed</u>!

3) Have I been empowered as the mouth, hands, and feet of Jesus on this earth to push back against the forces of darkness? Am I living that out in my daily life?

Well Sam, how does one do that? How does one become a "Christian Soldier" fighting back the power and plan of satan?

When I was a kid, in church, I remember pictures like this. My fellow Sunday School munchkins and I symbolically gathering behind Jesus on the way to victory.

But that was just a metaphor for being a Christian, right? I wasn't actually expected to become a spiritual warrior, was I?

That business of "putting on the armor of God" *(Ephesians 6:10-18)* is just a mental image about putting on character, spreading the Good News, and carrying and using your Bible, the Sword of the Spirit. Right?

Surely that's not actually suggesting that we are some kind of a Christian soldier in the middle of some cosmic battle between good and evil, is it?

Most of you who have walked with God *(and reached chapter five in this book)* would probably say: **"Yes, Sam, we are soldiers in the fight against evil. We are to be daily involved in pushing back the forces of darkness. We are supposed to be involved in Spiritual Warfare!"**

- But what does that actually mean?
- In what way was your life, this last week, part of some cosmic spiritual battle between good and evil, between God and satan?

We DO get the fact that **there is a war** for good and evil going on around us. Don't we? *(It's so vivid right now!)* We see the forces of evil seemingly gaining ground in many parts of our planet.

We DO get the fact that Jesus ripped away the keys of death and hell from satan effectively defeating him. We instinctively know humanity's sin price has been paid and forgiveness, redemption, and transformation are available to "whosoever will". We instinctively know *(and we know in detail from the pages of Scripture)* that **satan, and the forces of evil, are still in an all-out war for the souls of humanity**!

We've all experienced that horrendous lurch toward sin in our own lives. We all cry out to God when we see satan's evil pull in the lives of our children and grandchildren.

> But the idea that you and I are actually in place as one of God's warriors – that we *(as insignificant as we all feel)* **are chosen by God to push back against the forces of evil that are raging all around us on this planet and ACTUALLY WIN OVER THEM** is an idea that eludes many Christians.

As we have already studied:

- Many of us see our roles as defensive.

- Our task each day is to dodge satan's fiery darts of temptation.
- If we make it through the day, we will slump into our overstuffed chair, thankful that we have been victorious over the evil one – in that he hasn't spiritually squashed the life out of us!

We'll be content with a defensive posture with satan, and we'll leave the offensive role over the devil and the forces of evil to _____? **To whom? Whose job is it, to push back against the evil one?**

Does anybody seriously believe that phrases like "overwhelming victory," "more than a conqueror," "those who are victorious will sit with me on my throne just as I was victorious" – are talking about a defensive posture with sin and satan? If I can keep satan from tripping me up with my pet sin of _____ until I breathe my last breath, I will be "more than a conqueror." Really? *(I need to be careful not to diminish the importance of the above, it is important!)*

The Bible does, of course, mention the need to resist satan *(and his fiery darts)*, but it consistently puts you in an offensive posture over satan. And *(look closely)* **you are always presented as the favored victor!**

Submit yourselves, then, to God. Resist the devil, and he will flee from you.
James 4:7

As a child of God, as one who has been redeemed by the victory Jesus already won on the cross, **you start the battle with an overwhelming advantage!**

1) Submit yourself to God,

2) resist the devil,

3) and he will flee from you!

If the above statement is true, you have enormous divine power, through the shed blood of Jesus, to drive satan and his minions away from your life, your family, your friends, your church, your community, your state, your nation, and your world!

The only thing that would put you in a position to "not send satan packing" from your life circumstances, and from the life circumstances of those around you, would be if you...
_____What? **"If I had not confessed the sin in my heart, the Lord would not have listened. But God did listen! He paid attention to my prayer."** *(Psalm 66:18, 19)*

- We often do have sin issues in our life caused by the deceitful tricks of satan, but it is always and only because we have not taken advantage of the provisions of God's grace!

- God has been pouring grace in our direction! God is far more interested in your spiritual success than you are!

- He wants nothing else for you, but that you will spend all of eternity communing in his presence and "reigning" alongside him!

God set us up to be victorious over the evil one! He positions people and circumstances around us, to fall under the influence of our victorious, overcoming resistance over satan and his minions.

This sheds a new <u>negative</u> light on hiding in some corner hoping satan doesn't hit us with one of his "fiery darts," doesn't it?

We are, in fact, designed and called to be using the power God has given us to push back the forces of evil around us!

Please hear me:

1) The key by which you, the Believer, can take on the forces of darkness and push them back:

2) The key by which you, as part of Christ's Body, can smash the victory of Jesus' death and resurrection directly into the face of the evil one:

3) The key by which you, in the quiet corner of your home, can bring about lasting eternal change in this world, is prayer!

4) You, little insignificant you, *(and insignificant me)*, have the power to break the chains of the evil one over our family!

5) We have it within our grasp to turn back the tide of evil in our community!

6) You can pray for, and live to see, a revival that could transform the course of your nation from its hell-bent rush away from God – back toward "humbling ourselves and praying and seeking God's face, and turning from our wicked ways," and **God hearing our prayers from heaven and God healing our land!** (*2 Chronicles 7:14*)

Chess, you're overstating what prayer is all about! <u>Am I</u>?

- "Prayer is only about us coming to God with whatever might be on our minds, asking God for things in our lives, to which God will answer yes, no, maybe, or wait?" *(That is what is known in theological terms as "a bunch of hooey.")*

- I don't want to diminish the importance of bringing every need to God, no matter how small, or to overlook the fact that God uses our prayers, sometimes, to adjust our thinking to match his divine plan.

 But think about the prayers we prayed this last week. If our prayers were limited to: "God help me to have a good day and get everything done. Help Aunt Sadie control her cat. Help Uncle Fred not to spit so much when he talks" – we're seriously missing something!

But, **if prayer is somehow part of the great cosmic battle against the forces of sin and evil in this world**, enforcing the victory Jesus already won on the cross, now that's something else entirely!

Weak prayers are like going into battle with a butter knife. There's nothing wrong with a butter knife if you are spreading butter. But if you are looking to win in the battle against the evil one, **you might need a weapon that is mighty through God to the pulling down of strongholds!**

- When Jesus left here saying, "all authority in heaven and earth has been given to him," and "He would be with us always, even to the end of the age";

- When he said those who overcome will reign with him;

- When he said he would give the Church the "keys of the kingdom";

- When he said whatever the Church binds on earth will be bound in heaven;

- When Paul said don't you know that Christians will judge the world;

- When Paul said "if we endure with him we will also reign with him";

- **God was trying to get us to understand our "larger than life" role on this earth!**

God entrusted to those who, in the centuries to come, would embrace his gift of salvation, the task of "enforcing Jesus' victory" on the cross over sin and satan!

This is kind of sobering because each of us needs to look back over this last week and ask ourselves, **which of my prayers this last week would fall into the category of "enforcing God's will on this earth"?** If it's true that the average Christian prays less than five minutes a day and most of those prayers are

"God I need" prayers, chances are there is not a whole lot of "enforcing what God has already bound in heaven" getting done!

I'm not writing this to make us feel bad. *(I will be feeling bad too!)* Instead I'm writing this to startle us awake to what is actually available to us, to make us thirsty to experience a much deeper "warrior" prayer life than anything we have ever known!

Spiritual awakenings in the past 200 years have tended to last 40 - 80 years and have changed whole countries back in the direction of God's truth, his Word. Revivals, Awakenings, and Reformations on a massive scale seem to move like a divine fire from town to town, from country to country, spiritually igniting each person they touch.

Every time that has ever happened in history, it happened in response to fervent, almost desperate prayer! Imagine if revival were to happen in your town.

What if several churches in your town, humbled themselves, prayed, sought God's face, and turned from their wicked ways.

What if it ignited a revival spirit that spread across your city and region?

What if that happened in 50,000 towns across your country? What if a true spirit of revival were to spread from 50,000 different locations, all at the same time?

In September 1857, Jeremiah Lanphier started a prayer meeting in the upper room of the Dutch Reformed Church in Manhattan. In response to a newspaper ad, only six people out of a New York City population of one million showed up. But the following week there were fourteen, and then twenty-three. They then decided to meet every day for prayer. By late in the winter, they were filling the Dutch Reformed Church, then the Methodist Church on John Street, and then Trinity Episcopal Church on Broadway. In February and March of 1858, every church and public building in downtown New York was filled.

Horace Greeley, a famous New York Tribune news editor, sent a reporter on horse and buggy to the prayer meetings to count how many people were praying. In one lunch hour, he managed to get to only twelve of the meetings, but he counted 6,100 people in attendance.

But then a landslide of prayer began. It overflowed into the churches in the evenings. People began to be saved, ten thousand a week in New York City alone.

The revival spread throughout New England. Church bells brought people to prayer at eight in the morning, twelve noon, and six in the evening. The awakening extended up the Hudson and down the Mohawk where the Baptists, for example, had so many people to baptize that they went down to the river, cut a hole in the ice, and baptized them in the freezing water!

When the revival reached Chicago, a young shoe salesman went to the superintendent of the Plymouth Congregational Church and asked if he could teach Sunday School. The superintendent said, "I am sorry, young man. I have sixteen teachers too many, but I will put you on the waiting list." The young man insisted:

"I want to do something now." "Well, start a class." "How do I start a class?" "Get some boys off the street. They will be your class." He took them to a beach on Lake Michigan and he taught them Bible verses and Bible games, then he took them to the Plymouth Congregational Church. The name of the young man was Dwight Lyman Moody, and that was the beginning of his ministry that lasted forty years.

There were an estimated one million people who came into a relationship with Jesus Christ in that revival when the total population of the United States was only 30 million!

Might there be a "Jeremiah Lanphier" reading this book today?

Let's make sure we all understand what is really at stake here:

- John Wesley said, "God will do nothing except in answer to prayer." *Nothing?*
- E. M. Bounds said, "God shapes the world through prayer." *Really?*

So God is sitting up there in heaven, unable or unwilling to accomplish anything of significance on this earth until we get "on the horn" and ask him to do so? Be careful how you answer because there is some rich truth here:

1) God does not need us to convince him to act righteously on this earth.

2) We must not see ourselves as twisting the arm of God to do what he is unwilling to do, without our arm-twisting.

3) Prayer does not "influence" God, God is sovereign! He is all powerful and all knowing.

4) But what if: <u>God himself initiates all prayer</u>! Our prayers start in the mind and heart of God. When God sets up a course of action in this world, he looks for a person on whom he can lay the burden of prayer. One who will cooperate with him by fervently voicing the request back to him.

5) Why that's silly, why would God need our prayers to act? <u>He doesn't need our prayers to act</u>! <u>We need to pray</u>! It's part of our "apprenticeship" in enforcing the victory of Jesus!

We are training for reigning!

Prayer is not about us convincing God to do things. <u>It's all about us overcoming the evil one</u>! By the time a real burden of prayer consumes you, you can be sure that God is already mobilizing all the forces of heaven. If we understand this, and believe it, it will lead us to much greater faith!

It's not unlike a two-signature check. All of heaven's resources are behind the check.

Jesus has signed the check with his blood!

But until we walk into the Throne Room and also sign our name on the check, the resources remain untapped! Really? Yes, really!

- That's not our plan, it's God's plan!
- We just need to get more and more comfortable living out God's divine plan!

WHAT SCARES DEMONS: Part III

Chapter 6

"Our weapons have Divine power to
demolish strongholds!"

We've covered a lot of ground. Let me condense it into three concentrated statements:

#1) Salvation from the bondage of sin in my life is a matter of repenting and opening the "door of my heart" to Jesus. But then, my continued "victorious overcoming" of sin and satan in this life will prepare me to "sit with Jesus on his throne" in the eternal life to come! My future "reigning with Christ" is directly linked to my "victorious overcoming" in this life!

#2) Our "victorious overcoming" becomes a <u>life calling by God to be one of his spiritual warriors</u>, to push back against the forces of evil that are raging all around us on this planet and ACTUALLY WIN OVER THEM! We have enormous divine power, through the shed blood of Jesus and the power of his resurrection, to drive satan and his minions away from our life, our family, our friends, our church, our community, our state, our nation, and our world!

#3) It's through the process of <u>learning to "victoriously overcome" in this life</u>, that we go through the training of "learning to reign with Christ" in the life to come! *Are we hearing what God is saying to us?*

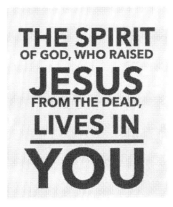

Are **YOU** hearing the message God is communicating to you personally? This truth has the power to change every day for the rest of your life!

It is the power of God, living in you that opens up in your life the "spiritual authority" to change the world around you! *(Romans 8:11)*

Let me recap this whole unfolding "theology of overcoming" in 82 words:

1) God created humanity to love and commune with.

2) God gave humankind dominion over the earth.

3) We rejected God and transferred that dominion to satan.

4) God incarnate, Jesus, came to earth to redeem us from sin.

5) He paid our sin penalty, he wrestled the dominion back from satan.

6) All authority in heaven and earth was given to Jesus, he said so!

7) And Jesus then gave us/me/you, his redeemed children, the authority to "enforce" the victory he already won on the cross!

That's a great big chunk of what our Christian life is all about! The Christian life isn't about accepting the faith of your parents, dragging yourself to church for an hour a week, giving the occasional dollar in the offering plate, and praying that God will overlook your sin, and graciously let you slip through "The Pearly Gates."

- In the real Biblical Christian life, you are to be a warrior, an over-comer, a Christian soldier! This isn't me being sensational. We've looked at passage after passage that says that very thing, in those very words.
- You have been commissioned and empowered by God to take on the enemy of God – and win!

Ephesians 6:10-12: "A final word: Be strong in the Lord and in his mighty power. Put on all of God's armor so that you will be able to stand firm against all strategies of the devil. For we are not fighting against flesh-and-blood enemies, but against evil rulers and authorities of the unseen world, against mighty powers in this dark world, and against evil spirits in the heavenly places."

Ephesians 6:10-12: "And that about wraps it up. God is powerful, and he wants you powerful. So take everything the Master has set out for you, well-made weapons, and put them to use so you will be able to stand up to everything the Devil throws your way. This is no afternoon athletic contest

that we'll walk away from and forget about in a couple of hours. This is for keeps, a life-or-death fight to the finish against the Devil and all his angels." *(The Message)*

We had the Vaughn family at our church a few years ago. They were talking about their Seal Team Six son, Aaron, who was shot down in Afghanistan. His mom, Karen, described the intense process that Aaron went through to rise to a position in one of the most elite fighting forces in the world. So when it was time to take out the number one terrorist in the world, Osama bin Laden, nobody had to mull over which group to deploy. Seal Team Six topped the list.

You are being called to that on a spiritual level!

- According to all the Scriptures we have been looking at, you are called, in-filled, empowered, and already deployed, as one of God's elite, overcoming warriors!
- Some of you are perhaps reading these words and are thinking no way – not me!!
- Some people who have been Christians for years, forever see themselves as still in some kind of a spiritual pre-military teen boot-camp.
- "I've been a Christian since 1952, and I'm still learning to shine my boots and present my Sword of the Spirit with the sharp end pointing away from me."

- Some "senior" Christians see themselves as already sitting over at the spiritual VFW building, talking about <u>what was, or what might have been</u>.

I was talking to a fairly young retired Christian, and said: "Do you realize that if you could get hold of the concept of yourself as a present-day spiritual warrior, and prayer as your spiritual weapon of choice, you could push back against the forces of sin and darkness in your family, and many of our families as well.

"With the time, and focus, that you have available *(that many of the younger families just don't have)*, if you just spent half an hour a day grabbing hold of heaven for the needs of others..." I finished up with something like, "You have the possibility and power to have more spiritual impact on this world than I do, standing at the pulpit, preaching sermons!"

1) Our weapons are not human weapons - we do not wage war as the world does.

2) Our "weapons" have Divine power, they are Mighty through God!

3) These weapons will demolish strongholds! *(2 Corinthians 10:4)*

- How often when we get ready to "say our prayers" do we think, "I'm entering into spiritual warfare with the evil one, and all his minions of darkness?"

- And yet **"my small, meager, human prayer"** has the **authority to turn the tide of evil back** from my family, my church, my community, my nation, and my world?

Do we believe that?

That is the theme from which Jesus' beginning "charter of the Church" comes:

> **Matthew 16:18-19: "I will build my church, and the <u>gates of Hell/Hades will not overcome it</u>.** *(In fact, my Church will learn to overcome the gates of hell!)* **I will give you/me/us (the Church) <u>the keys of the kingdom</u> of heaven;** *(What?)* **whatever you bind on earth <u>will have been bound in heaven</u>, and whatever you loose on earth <u>will have been loosed in heaven</u>!"** *How do we go about the binding and loosing on earth what has already been bound and loosed in heaven?*

This is, again, not me sensationalizing the Christian life. This is one of the New Testament's great promises right from the mouth of our Savior. Do we see a difference in the way Jesus looks at our **R**edeemed lives, and the way we often look at our **r**edeemed lives!

In order for any of this to play out in my life, I have to first buy into the fact that it is even possible.

- Maybe you still just can't see yourself as part of the active battle against evil. You still can't imagine that YOU are "called to enforce the victory that Jesus Christ already won on the cross."

- When Jesus promised in Revelation 3:21 that "those who overcome in this life will reign with Christ and sit with him on his throne just as he, Jesus, overcame, and sits with His Father on his throne," that surely has to be talking about somebody other than you? <u>Maybe in this great battle against evil you are called to be a civilian</u>? *Huh?*

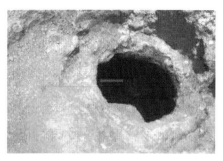 Remember dear old <u>Gideon</u>? God had a job for him to do defeating the evil enemies of Israel. Gideon was hiding out in the bottom of the winepress, hoping to stay an "unnoticed civilian." He was hiding from the Midianite raiders and any possibility of tangling with them.

Judges 6:12: "The angel of the LORD appeared to him and said, '<u>Mighty hero, the LORD is with you!</u>'"

Say what? Whoever you are looking for Mr. Angel Man, it isn't the guy hiding in the bottom of the wine press! "Oh yes; **MIGHTY HERO!** You are the right guy!" I'm not a hero, I'm not mighty, and I don't particularly believe the Lord is with me! *(How do we know that? Because Gideon says so!)*

Judges 6:13: "Sir," Gideon replied, "if the LORD is with us, why has all this happened to us? And where are all the miracles our ancestors told us about? Didn't they say, 'The LORD brought us up out of Egypt'? But now the LORD has abandoned us and handed us over to the Midianites."

Anybody ever look around yourself and feel like you are "abandoned to the Midianites," and the safest place for you is as far from any battle as you can possibly be?

Many of us discern that our whole world is in a pitched battle against the evil one right now! *(It's scary, and exhausting!!)* "So let's not just hang out around the winepress, let's climb inside and hide in the bottom of it!" Yes? No!

Judges 6:14: "Then the LORD turned to him and said, 'Go with the strength you have, and rescue Israel from the Midianites. I am sending you!'"

- What "strength I have"? I don't have any "strength"! There is "no strength in me"!

- I am sending you! Don't you get it Gideon? **I AM sending you!** You are a warrior, not because you were trained to be, not because it is in your genes, but because I am sending you!

- You are <u>a mighty hero</u>, not because you have ever done anything to deserve that title, but because you are about ready to walk out in the power of God, and fulfill the mission for which you were put on this earth!

Your calling is my calling!
I am the "Sending One"!

Judges 6:15: "'<u>But Lord</u>,' Gideon replied!" We all know the rest of the story: the fleeces, the reduction in soldiers down to just 300, **the mighty victory** and **that came not because of Gideon, but because of God!**

That's the lesson for every one of us reading this book who recoil at the mere thought that we can be used by God to battle back the forces of darkness in our world. We need to hear the voice of God in our ears:

1) Come on Mighty Heroes – Mighty Warriors!
2) Go in the strength you have been given!
3) The Lord is sending you!
4) The Lord is with you!
5) And everybody together says…

"But LORD"?!

What if it is true that the praying Church is actually deciding the course of human events? **What if the Church is the key that turns the lock to transforming the world for righteousness?**

- That is kind of the whole point in the Epistles of the New Testament, and that's exactly what the Early Church did!

- When you are praying, you are not only acting as a warrior of God against evil,

- When you are praying you are on the knife point, you are at the front edge of the bayonet!

- When you are praying, you are the hollow point tip of the bullet against satan and evil!

114

You can do more than pray, after you have prayed, but you cannot do more than pray until you have prayed.

John Bunyan – English Pastor
Author of "Pilgrims Progress"

Probing Premise # 1) If in fact true prayer originates in heaven. If prayer isn't us coming up with some bright idea and pummeling God until we can convince him to come around   to our way of thinking.

Probing Premise # 2) If it's true that God originates true prayer and then he looks for one of us, his children, his Church, on whom he can place the burden of prayer – who will be the tip of the spear to voice the request in faith, believing, back to Him.

Probing Premise # 3) That would certainly explain how "what you bind on earth will have already been bound in heaven; whatever you loose on earth will have already been loosed in heaven," wouldn't it? *(Matthew 16:19, Matthew 18:18)*

Probing Question # 4) If you knew that you were, literally, a key player in the huge, cosmic battle between the mighty power of God, and the soon to be defeated forces of sin and satan.

Probing Question # 5) If you really saw yourself as a warrior right out on the front lines.

Probing Question # 6) If you knew that your prayers could so smash the plans of satan that whole sinful campaigns that he has put in place to trip up your family, or church, or community, or country, or this world would come crashing down in response to your prayers.

> *Would it be worth the investment*
> *to fall on your knees and*
> *cry out to God?*

Probing Question # 7) If you really believed that your prayers were going to destroy satan's plans in reference to that person in your family that you are so concerned about.

Probing Question # 8) If you really believed that you could foil the plans of satan and literally bring his evil strategies to a standstill.

Probing Question # 9) If you really believed that your prayers would release the mighty power of God to do in your community what God has already foreordained in heaven. But its manifestation is waiting completely, totally, on people like yourself calling on God until you see the answer.

Probing Question # 10) If you really believed that our nation could be completely turned around until it, once again, is centered on God and his Word and that your great-grandkids could grow up in a much more righteous environment than you did.

If we really believed that with all our hearts – how much time would we be willing to invest in fervent prayer to God, until we saw it all unfold?

 What if prayer, really is like a safe deposit box with all the resources of heaven in it? Everything the world needs, everything your family needs, everything your church needs is there waiting to be tapped?

- God is standing by the box with his key already inserted in the first lock on the box.
- All that is needed to unlock the mighty resources of heaven is for us to insert the key we have been given, that key of powerful, effective, God-filled prayer!

The almost inconceivable scenario is for all that to be true and God to be standing there with the infinite Keys of the Kingdom waiting **and the "Redeemed Son or Daughter," just doesn't bother to show up with the second key!**

———————————

Here's one thing that is plaguing me. We have already studied that satan has effectively been defeated by Jesus' death and resurrection. His power over us is limited to bluff, and deception. <u>He can't make us do anything</u>! He can only deceive us into thinking we have to fall for his evil tricks. *(Of course those who have not embraced Christ's free gift are still firmly under satan's control!)*

- But it is the task of the Church who have been given "the keys to the kingdom" to "bind what has already been bound in Heaven"!

- It is the task of the Church to push back the plans and strategies of satan until he is sent fleeing, exactly as James 4:7 promises!

- We put on the "whole armor of God" **so that "<u>we can stand against</u> the schemes of the devil"!**

However, in the strategy planning rooms of hell, what do you think the first item on satan's agenda probably is?

1) Let's get every Christian to rob a bank and we will effectively shut down the advance of the Gospel. No?

2) Let's get every Christian to believe the lie that they are living on the edge of spiritual defeat all the time, and don't have enough spiritual power to keep their head above water, let alone worry about anyone else! *(Now that's more of a logical strategy, but I don't think it is at the top of satan's list.)*

3) Let's convince Christians that even though their spiritual lives are humming along pretty well, their relationship with the evil one is one of defense, always barely dodging his "fiery darts." When these Christians pray, their prayers need to be centered around them just getting through the next day.

4) "Let's entirely rob the Christians of the picture of themselves as warriors, on the offense against sin and satan. **All we have to do to foil the plans of God is to keep Christians from praying aggressively!"**

5) So how are we going to keep the Christians from praying?

a) Keep them too busy thinking about robbing a bank? No!

b) Keep them praying self-centered "I need" prayers? Maybe!

c) Lure them into the trap of putting everything else ahead of a focused, warrior prayer time. Simply keep them too distracted to pray, day after day, week after week, year after year. Yep!

"Every Christian we can keep focused on the temporal and mundane will keep them from defeating us in the realm of the eternal!" – satan

Don't attempt any more activity in your daily lives than you can immerse in fervent aggressive prayer!

Chapter 7

We're training for reigning!

This is chapter seven. We should probably make that the Biblical number of completion and bring this book to an end, but we have a lot to discuss yet!

In Jesus' final inspired revelation to humanity in Revelation chapter 3, Jesus is talking to the "lukewarm" church in Laodicea *(located in modern day Turkey)*. He's telling them they need to "heat up" in their relationship with him or face losing that relationship altogether. *("You have grown so shallow that I'm going to spit you out of my mouth," he said. Tough words to a once thriving, on-fire church!)* Then Jesus reviews exactly what he expects from the life of every Christian, every disciple of Christ! All who would ever follow him! There are two parts:

#1) Opening the door to Jesus by inviting him in as your Savior and as the Lord of your life, that's salvation! That's where each of us who have started on a spiritual journey with the God of the Universe began. Opening the closed door of our souls, and inviting Jesus to wash and cleanse our sinful hearts. That's Revelation 3:20.

> Revelation 3:20-21: "'Here I am! I stand at the door and knock. If anyone hears my voice and opens the door, I will come in and eat with that person, and they with me. To the one who is victorious, I will give the right to sit with me on my throne, just as I was victorious and sat down with my Father on his throne.'"

#2) What many often tend to miss is that <u>verse 21 is a fast forward to the end of your Christian life</u>, just as you breathe your last breath and show up in heaven. "St. Peter at the Pearly Gates" apparently isn't going to be so much focused on how financially successful you were on this earth, or how high you rose in influence and power.

- The big question each of us are going to have to answer is: "Did you OVERCOME while on this earth? Were you victorious?"
- It is not: "Did you overcome that strange clicking noise in your Chevy? Did you overcome by losing that stubborn extra 25 pounds"?
- This is a huge deal because it applies to every single follower of Jesus when you finish this life, and arrive in the hereafter.

Did you OVERCOME while living out your Christian life during your years on this planet? Remember, the answer to that question is very, very important because Jesus himself says that those who live their redeemed life here as "victorious overcomers" will "sit with him on his throne" in heaven!

Is that just a metaphor? Or will you actually be "reigning" over something, or somebody, when you get to heaven? We need to take the few minutes necessary to establish this as Biblical truth because this is what the Bible says will define our future when we stand in Heaven's Throne Room.

> **2 Timothy 2:11-12: "Here is a trustworthy saying: If we died with him, we will also live with him; if we endure, we will also reign** (συμβασιλεύω, symbasileuo, reign over, become rulers) **with him."** *You/me reigning with Jesus! Over who? Over what?*

> **Revelation 5:9-10: "And they sang a new song, saying: 'You (Jesus) are worthy to take the scroll and to open its seals, because you were slain, and with your blood <u>you purchased for God persons from every tribe and language and people and nation</u>. You have made them to be a kingdom and priests to serve our God, and <u>they will reign on the earth</u>.'"** *(βασιλεύσουσιν)*

This is not talking about this present moment in time. Revelation 5 is the great introduction to Revelation 6 where Jesus begins to open the seven seals which will all happen at the "end of time," the "end of the age."

It's the end of the world as we know it, and the beginning of eternity to come. Revelation 5 tells us, **"You purchased for God persons from every tribe and language and people and** nation. You have made them *(the purchased people)* to be a kingdom and priests to serve our God, and they *(we/us)* will reign on the earth." *(Did you know those verses were in the Bible?)*

> 1 Corinthians 6:1-3: "When one of you has a dispute with another believer, how dare you file a lawsuit and ask a secular court to decide the matter instead of taking it to other believers! Don't you realize that someday we Believers will judge the world? And since you are going to judge the world, can't you decide even these little things among yourselves? Don't you realize that we will judge *(evil)* angels?"

If you were to run those phrases by many, many Christians, they would say I never heard that before in my life. As it turns out, it's been right here in the book of 1 Corinthians for the last 1965+ years!

Let's cement this with one more Scripture, and then we'll move back to our "overcoming" theme. In the third chapter from the end of the Bible:

> Revelation 20:3-4 "The angel threw him (satan) into the bottomless pit, which he then shut and locked so Satan could not deceive the nations anymore until the thousand years were finished. Afterward he must be released for a little while. *(And then he will be put in the lake of fire forever!)* Then I saw thrones, and the people sitting on them had been given the authority to judge. And I saw the souls of those who had been beheaded for their testimony about Jesus and for proclaiming the

word of God. They all *(not just the martyrs)* **came to life again, and they reigned** (ἐβασίλευσαν) **with Christ for a thousand years."** To he or she who overcomes, I will grant to sit with me on my throne. It's not a metaphor, it is describing your future! *Do we all see that?*

Clearly a question that should pop into everybody's mind is: Who in the world are we going to be reigning over? Sorry; we're not going to answer that question in this book. I wrote about that in detail in the book **"Unmasking Revelation."**

But, to get to that promised "reigning" part of your future, Jesus says you need to be OVERCOMERS in this life! Not to beat on a dead horse, but who are we supposed to be "overcoming"?

Let's bring back six points *(slightly revamped)* from our last chapter to set our course. See if you can fill in the missing words:

1) Once we have repented and opened the "door of our heart" to Jesus, then our "victorious overcoming" over sin and satan in this life is preparing us to "sit with Jesus on his throne" in the eternal life to come! My "reigning with Christ" is directly linked to my "victorious overcoming" in this life! *(So says Jesus!)*

2) Our "victorious overcoming" becomes our spiritual life calling by God *(to do what?)* to be one of God's spiritual _____to push back against the forces of _____ that are raging all around us on this planet, and ACTUALLY WIN OVER THEM!

124

THE SPIRIT OF GOD, WHO RAISED **JESUS** FROM THE DEAD, **LIVES IN YOU**

3) Scripture says the Believer (you) has enormous divine power, through the shed _____ of Jesus and the power of his resurrection to drive _____ and his minions away from your life, your family, your friends, your church, your community, your state, your nation, and your world!

4) Jesus' victory on the cross, and in rising from the _____, gave us/me/you, his redeemed children, the authority to _____ the victory he won on the cross!

5) It's the power of God, living in you, that opens up in your life, the "spiritual authority" to spiritually _____ the world around you!

6) It's through the process of <u>learning to "victoriously overcome"</u> in this life that we go through the apprentice-ship of "learning to reign with Christ" in the life to come, in _____! *(We're more than conquerors, that's what the Apostle Paul calls us!)* **We're training for reigning!**

Taking two of the classic passages that describe what our spiritual life here on earth is supposed to be like, I personalized them. I'd like you to read them, forcefully, as a battle cry! *I might insert a few comments as we go along.* ☺

Ephesians 6:10-12: "I<u> am strong in the Lord and in his mighty power</u>! I am putting on all of God's armor so that I will be able to stand firm against all strategies of the devil!"

- I am not fighting against flesh-and-blood enemies.
- I'm fighting against evil rulers and authorities of the unseen world.
- I am fighting against mighty powers in this dark world.
- I am fighting against evil spirits in the heavenly places.

Did you notice we repeated the "I am fighting" phrase in all three sentences, because that is the actual meaning of the verse. In Greek, ἔστιν ἡμῖν ἡ πάλη, we are fighting, struggling, wrestling!

Did anybody reading this ever wrestle in school? You just keep on struggling for advantage. You never give up unless you get hopelessly pinned down – and the message of Scripture is that you, the Believer, won't have to get hopelessly pinned. **In fact, you are the one who is empowered to do the pinning!**

> Verse 13 goes on to say: **So put on the armor of God!** That word is a Greek "aorist imperative." You put God's armor on, and then you must carry it with you to the end of the battle which is the end of our lives!

> You put on the armor of God and **you leave it on!** When in your life can you lay down the Shield of Faith? When do you put the Sword of the Spirit in the closet and take some time off? You don't!

 The Roman enemies would light and shoot hollow oil-filled arrows, and if the arrow pierced a soldier, he would be covered with flames.

So the Romans developed large leather shields and soaked them in water. When the flaming arrows hit their shields, the fire would be extinguished.

The soldiers would stand side by side, front to back, and would hold up a wall of wet leather shields, and walk straight toward thousands of flaming arrows, looking through their peep hole.

When the enemy had shot their arsenal, the Romans would be right up against them where they could attack with their swords, knives, and clubs. Why do you think God would give that example to first century people? Because they all knew instantly, exactly, what the Scripture meant!

God wants his Christian warriors to lift their shield of faith and advance straight ahead into the battle. But we are not fighting against stinky, first century Barbarians, we are **fighting against evil rulers and authorities of the unseen world! We're fighting against mighty powers in this dark world! We are fighting against evil spirits in the heavenly places!** Amen?

Now; let's read this second classic verse in a "personalized" form:

2 Corinthians 10:3-4: "For though I live in the world, I do not wage war as the world does. The weapons I fight with are not the weapons of the world. On the contrary, <u>my weapons have divine power to demolish strongholds</u>."

- Clearly the weapons we fight with are **prayer** and the immensely powerful **<u>Word of God</u>**!

- I'm **entering into spiritual warfare with the evil one**, and all his minions of darkness, and yet **my "tiny, seemingly insignificant, meager, human" prayers have the authority to turn the tide of evil back!**

Again I challenge us all, me too!

1) What if I knew that I was, literally, a key player in the huge cosmic battle between the mighty power of God, and the soon to be defeated forces of sin and satan? What if I really saw myself as a warrior right out on the front lines?

2) What if I knew that my prayers could so smash the plans of satan that whole sinful campaigns that he has put in place to trip up my family, or my church, or my community, or my country, or my world would come crashing down in response to my prayers, would it be worth the investment to fall on my knees and cry out to God?

When I first preached this material in our church, I noticed that as the weeks progressed many people were really getting quite serious.

- The praying in our Tuesday night "War Room" prayer time took on a new fervency.
- The prayers in our leadership meetings took on a decided "warrior" flavor.
- Some said their private praying became far more aggressive, I know mine did!

- People were lifting their shield of faith and walking right toward the evil one swinging the Sword of the Spirit.

- **"Satan, you don't get to have our kids! Satan, you don't get to have our church. Satan, you don't get to disrupt our community. Satan, you don't get to destroy our nation!"**

- How seriously do we believe that? What are you willing to do about it?

The Coronavirus pandemic is still hanging over us as I write these words. This world-wide plague didn't come from God! A virus that shuts down human interaction world-wide – Really? A plague that stops people from human inter-connection, from showing affection, shaking hands, or hugging – things we literally all need for emotional survival.

A plague that shuts down churches, forbids million/billons of people from meeting to worship God, forbids us from gathering our children to train them in the Scriptures. Where do we think all of this is coming from?

In an unprecedented case like this, do we simply look at the daily case charts and wish it would go away, or do we, realizing the havoc it has brought on our communities and country, tug on heaven in fervent prayer until we see it retreat into oblivion?

This was such a big deal in 2020: One large state on our west coast was forbidding churches to meet in their buildings. Even forbidding them to have private Bible studies in their homes, and telling them if any three people do meet they can not sing because singing might transmit the disease!

Hebrews 10:23-25: "Let us hold tightly without wavering to the hope we affirm, for God can be trusted to keep his promise. Let us think of ways to motivate one another to acts of love and good works. And <u>let us not neglect our meeting together, as some people do</u>, but encourage one another, <u>especially now that the day of his return is drawing near</u>."

A well-known pastor, speaker, and author in the U.S. sent out a manifesto, where he stated "<u>enough is enough</u>"!

- Our large church is going to meet as instructed by Scripture.
- We're going to be careful, taking social distancing precautions, but we are going to meet, and yes, we are even going to sing praises to God.

Imagine a government in the U.S. arresting a Pastor for leading worship. Just think about that and let it sink in!

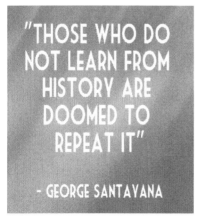

"THOSE WHO DO NOT LEARN FROM HISTORY ARE DOOMED TO REPEAT IT"

- GEORGE SANTAYANA

Does anybody remember the history of why the United States was founded? We specifically resisted those who would forbid religious liberty. **We wrote it into the first 16 words of our Bill of Rights!** "Congress shall make <u>no law respecting an establishment of religion, or prohibiting the free exercise thereof!</u>"

130

Does anybody remember the history of communist countries where churches were shut down, and the absolute horrifying carnage that followed?

Some of what we see going on around us on this earth <u>is not really being hatched in brightly lit boardrooms. It's being hatched in the boardrooms of hell</u>! So let me say this again:

1) If you knew that you were, literally, a key player in the huge cosmic battle between the mighty power of God, and the soon to be defeated forces of sin and satan, if you really saw yourself as a warrior, right out on the front lines,

2) If you knew that your prayers could so smash the plans of satan that whole sinful campaigns that he has put in place to trip up your family, or your church, or your community, or your country, or your world, would come crashing down in response to your prayers, would it be worth the investment to fall on your knees and cry out to God?

In the U.S., in the "horror show" that was the year 2020, it wasn't just Covid-19 that was shaking our nation. Our nation became unbelievably divided with not just peaceful protests, but with open violence and anarchy. Peaceful protests are part of the same first amendment that protects our freedom of religion. But what we were seeing in the form of violent destruction, burning down businesses, beating and killing people was not "peaceful protests."

I told our church, as a Pastor, with a heavy heart: "If we think we are just going over a small speed bump as a nation and soon tensions will die down, and everything will go back to normal and we will all move together toward a blessed national utopia, we are probably seriously misinformed.

- The evil one has a very special hatred for the USA! We're the only nation that was, literally, founded on the entire Word of God.
- Israel was founded on the Old Testament and the evil one has a very, very special hatred for that country as well.
- But the U.S., more than any other nation on the planet, was specifically founded on the Gospel of Jesus Christ!
- It was written into our laws. It was written into the fabric of our society.
- Satan wants, with every ounce of his evil being, to bring our country to its knees!
- **So, I asked our church: <u>Who exactly is going to stop the evil plans of satan for our nation</u>?**
- Is God counting on politicians to fix the problem? Or is he counting on the CHURCH to divinely, sovereignly fix the problem? *(Now, politicians who are part of Jesus' church, that's a very good plan!)*

We desperately need a mighty revival, a reformation, to sweep through this country bringing back the God-centered focus we once had!

But the only way a revival will come to this country is if the people of God fall on their face and submit themselves to the mighty will of God. **Then those same people must "resist the devil" with all the power within them from the indwelling Holy Spirit of God who raised Jesus from the dead!**

James 4:7 says: satan and his minions will be required to flee, not just from our lives, but from the lives of so many sin-chained people living around us that we will/must pray for!

Satan has a very well-thought-out, long-planned strategy for bringing my/our once-God-focused nation to its knees, and the only people God has empowered to stop satan in his tracks is us, the Redeemed!

You have power over sin and satan that nobody else is promised! You are one of God's victorious overcoming spiritual warriors!

Some of you might not be aware of the danger that is actually going on in your world. The leaders of the organizations who are stirring up anarchy and violence in the US in 2020 have openly claimed on public television, and on their websites, that they are "Marxist" trained. To some younger readers that doesn't mean a thing. But to you older people, it brings back vivid awful images.

- We remember Marxism/Communism's stated desire to take over the world. Many watched Communism take over country after country in Europe when you were younger. I can remember the constant threat that the communists were going to send nuclear bombs to wipe out the United States.

- And you that know your history know that Russian Marxist/Communist leader Vladimir Lenin, in his Red Terror, **killed as many as 20 million** of his fellow countrymen and put many more in concentration camps.

- Lenin was eclipsed by Marxist/Communist leader Joseph Stalin who violently **killed as many as 40 million** of his own fellow countrymen and women.

 But Marxist/Communist Chinese Chairman Mao in just four years from 1958 to 1962, in what he called the "Great Leap Forward," **executed 45 million of his own people** to gain total power. He did things like forcing fathers to bury their own children alive, torturing and killing whole families because one starving boy took some grain for food. Thousands of families were simply deprived of food till the whole family died of starvation. That's Marxism!

- **Marxism/Communism has executed more than 100 million** (100,000,000) **people in the last 100 years.** They were slaughtered by evil, evil people who held Marxism as their ideology!
- And now we have young leaders in this world who are proudly announcing that they want to take our world "forward" to the utopia of Marxism!

134

- Some of what we see going on around us on this earth is not really being hatched in brightly lit boardrooms. It's being hatched in the pit of hell!

Well Pastor Chess, how can somebody like me, a single unknown voice, have an impact on satan's worldwide plans to bring the "Christian" part of my country and world crashing to the ground?

Not only can you do it, you are the only ones God has called and empowered to do it!

You have far more going for you than the elected president of a country has. Let me show you:

In 2 Kings 6, the king of Aram was attacking Israel. But every time he made a secret plan on where to attack, the prophet Elisha would tell the king of Israel exactly what the king of Aram's military strategy was, and Israel's army would be there waiting! *(Nobody was telling Elisha. He was talking to God, and God was showing him!)*

> **2 Kings 6:11-13: "The king of Aram became enraged over this. He called his officers together and demanded, 'Which of you is the traitor? Who has been informing the king of Israel of my plans?' 'It's not us, my lord the king,' one of the officers replied. 'Elisha, the prophet in Israel, tells the king of Israel even the words you speak in the privacy of your bedroom!' 'Go and find out where he is,' the king commanded, 'so I can send troops to seize him.'"**

Ok, one little dude up against a powerful army, and the only weapon <u>Elisha had was the weapon of prayer</u>. Is it significant that God kept showing the "praying prophet" what the plans of the enemy were in time for him to foil them? Might God be willing to do that for us, for you?

2 Kings 6:14-15: "The report came back: 'Elisha is at Dothan.' So one night the king of Aram sent a great army with many chariots and horses to surround the city. When the servant of the Man of God got up early the next morning and went outside, there were troops, horses, and chariots everywhere. '<u>Oh, sir, what will we do now</u>?' the young man cried to Elisha."

Surrounded! The enemy is all around you!

Let's apply this to ourselves! If the enemy was only coming from the front you would hold up your shield of faith, and run in slicing and dicing with the Word of God! Yes? But now it seems like the enemy is coming from every side at the same time. You are surrounded by the minions of the evil one. What in the world are you going to do?

I'm going to say this gently, but firmly, as a Pastor. If there is not something deep inside of you telling you that our world is in the most serious spiritual crisis that any of us have ever experienced before, then perhaps we need more discernment because we are truly sitting on a precipice!

- As somebody who has spent hundreds, and hundreds, and hundreds of hours studying End Times,
- In my honest opinion, we are "careening" toward the End Times prophesied in the Bible!
- That's why I've been saying a lot that not only do we need to be resetting our lives to truly be God's Spiritual Warriors, but we better be training our children to be Generals and Colonels in the Army of the Lord! Anything less is eternally short-sighted!

But the situation is not even remotely hopeless. We are promised to be Overcoming Victors! We are promised to be "more than conquerors"! And every single one of us was positioned by God to be on this planet <u>at this exact moment in time</u>!

> **2 Kings 6:16: "'Don't be afraid!' Elisha told him. 'For there are more on our side than on theirs!'"** *(There are more with us than there are with them!)*

We sometimes think we are down here begging God to do something for us he may or may not be willing to do! That's not true! **God has given us the Keys of the Kingdom and is asking us to bind and loose on earth, what has already been bound and loosed in heaven!** *(Matthew 16:19)*

"Oh God, let us see things from your perspective!" God is not sweating about what is happening on this earth right now. He's not concerned about 20 years from now. He's timeless. He's already there! And he sees what we can't see!

2 Kings 16:17: "Then Elisha prayed, 'O LORD, open his eyes and let him see!' The LORD opened the young man's eyes, and when he looked up, he saw that the hillside around Elisha was filled with horses and chariots of fire!"

Jeremiah 32:18: "You show steadfast love to thousands, but you repay the guilt of fathers to their children after them, O great and mighty God, whose name is the Lord of Hosts (צָבָא, tsaba, army, war, warfare)." (The Lord of Heaven's Armies! *Very possibly/probably – the pre-incarnate Jesus!*)

When Jesus returns in his glorious Second Coming, all the armies of the world will be gathered around Jerusalem. *(Revelation 19:19)* Jesus will come to earth with the angels of heaven, but He won't even need them, He will destroy all the remaining hate-filled armies of the world with a sword/breath from his mouth. *(Revelation 19:21 Battle of Armageddon)*

We will have to stop for this chapter *(we'll come back to this account)*, but this next verse in the story may apply to our praying right about now:

2 Kings 6:18: "As the Aramean army advanced toward him, Elisha prayed, 'O LORD, please make them blind.' So the LORD struck them with blindness as Elisha had asked."

- Perhaps that is a good prayer to pray against the enemies of God;
- "Oh God, make them blind! Make them do things they think are so smart, but which actually lead them into their own defeat!"

WHAT SCARES DEMONS: Part IV

Chapter 8

Prayers outlive the lives of those who uttered them;
outlive a generation, outlive an age,
outlive a world. – E.M. Bounds

Let's review. Reviewing is good. Reviewing locks truth into our brain. But let's personalize this whole section so that our conscious mind picks up that this is not just written for Believers in general – but that these are specifically my personal truths:

Revelation 3:21: "To the one who is victorious, I will give the right to sit with me on my throne, just as I was victorious and sat down with my Father on his throne."

---

1) Once I have repented and opened the "door of my heart" to Jesus, then my "victorious overcoming" over sin and satan in this life is preparing me to "sit with Jesus on his throne" in the eternal life to come! My "reigning with Christ" is directly linked to my "victorious overcoming" in this life!

2) My "victorious overcoming" becomes my spiritual life calling by God to be one of God's spiritual warriors – to push back against the forces of darkness and evil that are raging all around me on this planet, and ACTUALLY WIN OVER THEM!

3) My weapons of choice are world shaping <u>PRAYER</u>, and surgically slicing into the sinful world around me with the "Sword of the Spirit," the intensely powerful Word of God!

- **What if** my prayers *(weak as I sometimes feel they are)*, **what if** the weakest prayers I pray are actually hugely powerful in the spirit world around me *(heavenlies)*?

- **What if** my prayers are indeed the weapon through which God has chosen for his Church to enforce his victory on the cross over satan in this present world? *(That absolutely is the case!)*

- **What if** it's actually true that real world changing prayer originates in Heaven? What if prayer isn't me coming up with some bright idea, and pummeling God until I convince him to come around to my way of thinking?

- **What if** it's true that God originates real prayer and then he looks for one of us, his children, his Church, on whom he can place the burden to pray – who will become the tip of the spear to grab hold of heaven and cry out to God in faith?

- **If I really believed** that my prayers were going to smash satan's plans in the life of that person in my family that I am so concerned about;

- **If I really believed** that I could foil the plans of satan and literally bring his evil strategies to a standstill;

- **If I really believed** that my prayers would release the mighty power of God to do in my family, or community, or nation what God has already fore-ordained in Heaven but He is waiting patiently on people like me, calling on him until I see positive answers.

- **If I really believed** that with all my heart, <u>how much time would I be willing to spend</u> in fervent, family changing, church changing, nation changing, world changing prayer until I saw it all unfold?

There are two Bible stories I want to unwrap in this chapter, one from the Old Testament and one from the New Testament. Both show us a clear picture of what is really going on in "the heavenlies," and how much we, the children of God, are supposed to be a massive cosmic influence.

o Many of us, when we pray, struggle to see our prayers as getting any further than the ceiling of the room where we are praying.

- What if that's not the way it really is at all? What if satan and his minions start to cringe when you begin a prayer?

- What if when you really buckle down and pray, words that push back the forces of darkness from around your family, community, and nation, and call out to unleash God's mighty power;

- What if your prayers actually cause satan and his fallen demons to shudder in terror? To flee as far away as they can get from the sound of your voice.

That's actually how the Bible describes God's power in the Followers of God, even in the Old Testament, but particularly in the New Testament Church! The power that Acts and the Epistles describe in the life of a spirit-filled, spirit-led Jesus Follower was/is truly awesome!

It really is! Acts 17:6 says those First Century people turned their pagan world upside down! How would you like that to be said of you?

Through his prayers, through her prayers, they turned their church, their community, and their nation upside down! Exchanging a sin-soaked atmosphere for a roaring flame of God's presence and power!

- But that's not me Sam. **Yes it is!** If you are a Believer!

- I don't/can't have that kind of spiritual power – **Yes you do/can**! The Bible doesn't draw any distinction from one Christian to the next!

- We just have to **get a new picture** *(the right picture)* in our minds of who we, the Redeemed, actually are in the mind of God.

> **"The Spirit of God, who raised Jesus from the dead, lives in you! And just as God raised Christ Jesus from the dead, He will give LIFE to your mortal bodies by this same spirit living within you!"** *(Romans 8:11)*

I would like to etch the following Old Testament snapshot into our minds, and then we'll move to the New Testament. We started this account in the last chapter. It is such an amazing story.

Remember our beginning look at 2 Kings 6 in chapter seven? The king of Aram was attacking Israel. But every time he made a secret plan on where to attack, the prophet Elisha would tell the king of Israel exactly what the king of Aram's military strategy was. And Israel's army would be there waiting to conquer him!

King Ben Hadad II is livid. "Who's the spy? Who's the traitor?" "Nobody, King Ben Hey-DAD! There's a prophet over in Israel whose God is telling him what you whisper in your bedroom!" *(By the way, 2 Kings 5 is where Elisha healed the*

Captain of Ben "Hey-Dad's" army. So maybe that is who is now doing the talking to the King.)

Ben Hadad sends his whole army to pick up one man! Try to grasp the stupidity of him thinking that he was going to sneak his whole army up on a man who knew everything he whispered in his bedroom. But he tried to do it anyway!

Elisha obviously knew he was coming, but is sleeping like a baby in perfect peace, trusting completely in the power of his God:

1) He had peace instead of panic! If God knows everything about the evil one's plans, wouldn't it be short-sighted to think he isn't way out ahead of anything the "principalities and powers" have schemed for your life right now!

2) He was "seeing the unseen"! Oh God open our eyes to see what you see!

2 Kings 6:15-17: "When the servant of the Man of God got up early the next morning and went outside, there were troops, horses, and chariots everywhere. 'Oh, sir, what will we do now?' the young man cried out to Elisha. '<u>Don't be afraid!</u>' Elisha told him. '<u>For there are more with us, than there are with them</u>!' *Where?* **Then Elisha prayed, 'O LORD, open his eyes and let him see!' The LORD opened the young man's eyes, and when he looked up, he saw that the hillside <u>around Elisha was filled with horses and chariots of fire</u>!"**

This is a really important picture to let consume our thinking:

146

- Here's pagan Ben-Hadad spending vast amounts of his tax-payers money to mobilize an army, and travel days and days, just to crush the man of God like a bug.
- He could have sent a couple of army Rangers to do the job, but as we have already said; "satan, and those who follow him, don't think logically *(theo-logically)!*"
- Satan is a liar, he is the father of lies. He lies all the time <u>even to himself</u>!

Imagine Ben-Hey-Dad's vast powerful army strutting their way toward Dothan to pick up one little prophet man. <u>And just above them, in the "fourth dimension" is a huge army of angels in chariots of fire just waiting for God's Word to extinguish his whole military force</u>.

One angel could have wiped out Ben-Hadad's whole elite force, but the Lord of Hosts sends along a whole vast army of powerful angels. *(Which made Hadad's Army seem like tiny cockroaches.)* Not because God needed them to do the job, but just to show Elisha's servant *(and all of us who would follow)* what God has available to deliver us in times of trouble!

o Picture the army of satan that you feel is often arrayed against you!
o **<u>Now lift your eyes up</u> and see the vast army of angels that God has commissioned to protect you!**
o They are hovering over satan, just waiting for God's Word *(perhaps as a result of your prayers)* to squash the evil enemy's army like a bug!

Psalm 34:7: "The angel of the Lord encamps around those who fear Him, and <u>he rescues them</u>!"

147

Psalm 91:11: "He will give his angels charge concerning you, to guard you in all your ways!"

PRAYER is designed to replace PANIC! Prayer opens our eyes to spiritual reality! Faith and fear can't occupy the same space at the same time!

2 Kings 6:18-19: "As the Aramean army advanced toward him, Elisha prayed, 'O Lord, please make them blind.' So the Lord struck the whole army with blindness as Elisha had asked."

Then Elisha *(The very man they were looking for)* went out and said, "Hey guys, **How's it going? Having a little trouble with your eyes**? Here, let me help you! You've actually come the wrong way! This isn't even the right city! Follow me, and I will take you to the man you are looking for." And he led them right into the capital city where the Israelite King and his army were! Then Elisha prayed the ole "God open their eyes prayer" again. And the Lord opened their eyes, and they found themselves right in the middle of Samaria!

2 Kings 6:21-23: "When the king of Israel saw them, he shouted to Elisha, 'My father, should I kill them? Should I kill them?' 'Of course not!' Elisha replied. 'Do we kill prisoners of war? Give them food and drink and send them home again to their master.' So the king made a great feast for them and then sent them home to their master. After that, the Aramean raiders stayed away from the land of Israel."

Fast forward, with me, to the New Testament. Satan doesn't back off in his efforts to defeat God and his children. *Remember*:

- When the evil one figures out that Jesus is God in human form on this earth;
- When Jesus himself states that he has come to bring all people into abundant life. "To seek and save those who are lost,"
- When Jesus leaves little doubt that he is the long-awaited Messiah described in Isaiah 53, who will take humanity's sins on himself;

Satan and his minions turn on every godless, evil scheme they can think of to stop God from achieving the ultimate victory. Jesus himself responds by alerting satan and his demons that he has prepared a lake of fire as the final home for them. Their fight to kill Jesus is one of utter desperation! But watch this important point:

God's reaction is to say: not only do I have an army of angels who can very effectively control the universe and bring my will to pass on earth, but…

- o I am also going to **raise up an army of Redeemed Saints on the earth!**
- o I'm going to raise that army up out of the same fallen humans that you, satan, have controlled for so long.
- o **Once these "saved Saints" learn just how much spiritual power they really have, they will become an awesome, unstoppable force of victorious over-comers!**

- Their learning to "overcome you" on this earth will prepare them to "reign with me in heaven" for all of eternity while you, satan, and your minions, roast forever in the lake of fire!

So Jesus raises up the Church. He tells his disciples his plans back in Matthew 16. And his plans for the Church are not just to save them from their sins, he is raising up his Church to combat the forces of the evil one! It will be their task to push back against the powers of darkness! **In so doing these Saved Saints (YOU/ME) will be "training for reigning"**!

1) <u>I am going to build my Church,</u>

2) <u>all the gates of hell/hades will not conquer it</u>. *(prevail, overpower it)*

3) I will give you (my church) the <u>keys of the kingdom.</u>

4) **<u>With those keys in hand</u> and my promise that the gates of hell will not overpower you!**

5) **Whatever you bind on earth** *(perfect passive participle)* **has <u>already been bound in heaven</u> and whatever you loose on earth has <u>already been loosed in heaven</u>!**

That's literally a definition of life changing, family changing, church changing, nation changing, world changing prayer!

- With the promise of God's protection from the evil one we literally take Jesus' keys of the kingdom, and with those keys in hand, we can begin to bind and loose on earth what has already been bound and loosed in heaven in prayer!

- **It's our task! It's our calling. It's our privilege!**

- Remember Jesus' Prayer to the Father: "Your kingdom come, your will be done, on earth as it already is in heaven?"

- <u>We</u> **are Jesus' solution to the Lord's Prayer coming to pass!** *(Loosing on earth what has already been loosed in heaven!)*

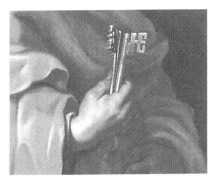

1) You, my church, will have the responsibility to determine what I have already sealed as my divine Kingdom plan in heaven.

2) You, my church, are the ones I have chosen to use the authority of the Kingdom keys I have given you to lock and unlock the power of heaven onto your fellow inhabitants on earth.

3) You, my Church, will have the privilege of advancing my Kingdom plan for this planet. Pushing back the very forces of sin and evil until the final culmination when I will return in my glorious Second Coming to set up my Heavenly Kingdom here on earth!

That's why I often say that the Early Church caught this reality so much better than we do. In the most hideously sinful culture, *(of human sacrifice, and obscene sexual perversions)* the hot button issues of today of abortion, euthanasia, sexual crimes against children, human slavery, sex slavery, women's rights, children's rights and on and on – <u>were in the worst possible ways, the absolute norms of ancient Roman society</u>!

The Early Church wasn't praying, "God help me to find the best deal on tires for my car," – but "God preserve my family from being murdered this week, and my children from being carted off as slaves to some pagan."

It was in that kind of a setting that the Church **used the keys of the kingdom to choke off satan's power over, and over, and over** until all of society, around them, started to change. Finally in 313 AD, Christianity became legal and the killing largely stopped.

Clement of Alexandria recorded: Wherever they went, Christians were opposed as anti-social, atheistic and depraved. Their message exalted a "crucified criminal," and nothing could have been more calculated than that to not win them converts.

But, when a **<u>devastating plague</u>** swept across the ancient world, *(sound familiar)* Christians were the only ones who cared for the sick. They did it at the risk of contracting the plague themselves. Meanwhile, the pagans were throwing infected members of their own families into the streets even before they died in order to protect themselves from the disease. *(Intimacy with God – Clement of Alexandria)*

Let me show you this very same thing in action in the Early Church. It's another amazing story!

<u>**Herod Agrippa, grandson of Herod the Great**</u> who had slaughtered all the babies in Bethlehem, thinks he is on a roll. The Herods were awful people who got their positions ruling over the Jews by kissing up to the Roman Emperor.

- The Jews hated them, but in the first century, they also hated the Christians. So Herod Agrippa, to make points with the Jews, started arresting the leaders of the Christian Church in Jerusalem.

- He slaps several in prison including Peter. Then in one grandiose move, he executes James, Jesus' disciple, the brother of John, the fishing partner of Peter and Andrew!

- He sliced off James' head with a sword which is a mode of death that Deuteronomy 13 says is only for those who are leading others away from Yahweh, God. Understand, that's what the Jews thought the Christians were doing, and that's probably why "old suck-up" Herod killed James that way.

- More importantly, to this account, Herod had Peter locked in prison and there was little doubt that he was going to be the next one to have his head sliced off!

Notice how serious Herod was taking this: He has posted four squads of four soldiers each. Two soldiers are chained to each of Peter's arms. Two more are standing guard at the door of Peter's cell. There is an iron gate leading out of the prison into the city beyond. Herod had arrested him right during Passover, and apparently planned to try and execute him thinking he would be riding at the top of his game by next week.

It's important to see that as we enter Acts chapter 12 with James dead and Peter in prison waiting to die. The church is in emotional turmoil because of what is suddenly happening, and **Herod is grinning from ear to ear thinking he's won the battle.**

We end chapter twelve with Peter out of prison, the church is once again thriving, and Herod is unexpectedly "deader than a doornail" having rotted from the inside out!

What happened in the middle of that massive one chapter shift that is notable for us right now?

Acts 12:5: "While Peter was in prison, the church prayed very earnestly for him."

Acts 12:7-9: "Suddenly, there was a bright light in the cell, and an angel of the Lord stood before Peter. The angel struck him on the side to awaken him and said, 'Quick! Get up!' And the chains fell off his wrists. Then the angel told him, 'Get dressed and put on your sandals.' And he did. 'Now put on your coat and follow me,' the angel ordered. So Peter left the cell, following the angel. But all the time he thought it was a vision. He didn't realize it was actually happening."

So Peter left the cell, following the angel. <u>But all the time he thought it was a vision. He didn't realize it was actually</u>

<u>happening</u>. *(Wait a minute, wouldn't Peter have been praying too? Where's your faith dude?)*

> Acts 12:10-11: "They passed the first and second guard posts and came to the iron-gate leading to the city, and <u>this opened for them all by itself</u>. So they passed through and started walking down the street, and then the angel suddenly left him. Peter finally came to his senses. 'It's really true!' he said. 'The Lord has sent his angel and saved me from Herod and from what the Jewish leaders had planned to do to me!'"

Remember Peter, It's called "loosing on earth (literally) what has already been loosed in heaven!"

"You, my church, will have the responsibility to determine what I have already sealed as my divine Kingdom plan in heaven!

You, my church, are the ones I have chosen to use the authority of the Kingdom keys I have given you to lock and unlock the power of heaven onto your fellow inhabitants on earth!" Jesus

- Peter races over to the house of Mary, John Mark's mom, where the prayer meeting was taking place. He knocks on the door. "Who is it," says Rhoda?

155

- "It's me," says Peter. Rhoda gets so flustered she leaves him outside and runs to tell everyone he is there. "You're nuts," they reply!

- Peter keeps banging on the door, he is after all a fugitive from the law. Finally, they let him in and are all amazed that he is free from his prison cell and the platoon of guards Herod had posted.

- He tells them all about the angel thumping him upside the head. Then he takes off to hide from Herod.

- There's a massive uproar when the guards find him missing. They search everywhere. Herod has all the poor innocent guards executed. Herod himself leaves Jerusalem *(in embarrassment, I would imagine)* and went to Caesarea where he met his doom.

Acts 12:21-24: "Herod put on his royal robes, sat on his throne, and made a speech to them. The people gave him a great ovation, shouting, 'It's the voice of a god, not of a man!'

Instantly, an angel of the Lord struck Herod with a sickness, because he accepted the people's worship instead of giving the glory to God. So he was consumed with worms and died. Meanwhile, the word of God continued to spread, and there were many new believers."

PRAYER replaced PANIC!

David Mikkelson wrote about a medical missionary to Africa who was speaking at his home church in Michigan. He told about how he often had to travel by bicycle through the jungle to a nearby city for supplies. It was a two-day trip that required camping overnight at the halfway point.

When he got to the city, he would go to the bank, get money, and buy medicine and supplies to take back. On one of these trips, he saw two men fighting. One had been badly injured, so the missionary treated his wounds, witnessed to him, and returned home without incident.

On his next trip to town, the man he had treated came up to him and said that he knew the missionary was carrying money and supplies. This man and some friends had, on his previous trip, followed him into the jungle, planning to kill him and take his money and drugs. But just as they were ready to move into his campsite, **they saw that he was surrounded by 26 armed guards.**

When the missionary heard this, he laughed and said that he was all alone out at that jungle campsite. But the man insisted, **"No, not only I, but also my five friends saw and counted the 26 guards. Because of them we were afraid and left you alone."**

At this point in the church in Michigan where the missionary was telling the story, a man jumped to his feet and asked, "Can you tell me the exact day this took place?" The missionary thought for a moment and was able to give the exact date.

The man in the church continued, "When it is night in Africa, it is morning here. That morning I was preparing to go play golf. As I was putting my golf bag in my car, I felt the Lord leading me to pray for you. This urging was so strong that I called the men in this church to meet here and pray for you. **Would all of those men who met with me on that day, please stand up?"** <u>All together, 26 men were standing</u>! *Published online: 09/18/2020*

- **Snopes** unconditionally rates the above story as <u>**false**</u> *("an embellished parable").*

- They also list several other similar stories, including one from Wesley Deuwel/Bill Bright's *"Touch the World through Prayer,"* 1986, and one from Billy Graham's book, *"Angels: God's Secret Agents,"* 1975, as false.

- **They dismiss them all as fables. <u>Do you</u>?**

Chapter 9

Prayer opens our eyes to God's reality!

I'm still focused on the amazing Bible account that we have been studying for the last two chapters. I want to take you back there one more time, briefly, in this last chapter, and then jam our finger on a reverse button to look at some amazing application truth that has lodged in my own egg-shaped head.

Remember, in **2 Kings 6** the king of Aram was attacking Israel. But every time he made a secret plan on where to attack, the prophet Elisha would know it and tell the king of Israel exactly what Ben-Hadad's military strategy was.

King Ben Hadad is so ticked off he sends an **entire army** to capture Elisha, which was stupid and illogical, because if Elisha knew every word he "whispered in his bedroom" *(as the text says)*, then he clearly knew the army was coming and could have easily been 100 miles away when they arrived!

But here's an important point, Elisha saw in his spiritual mind the huge lethal army approaching. He knew when they got within 5 miles of Dothan. He knew when they surrounded the city. But <u>rather than running in terror for his life, he was completely calm and unafraid</u>. Why?

Well, that's easy Chess, that's a major point of the story. Elisha's servant, when he saw the army, was scared out of his gourd! He screamed, "Oh Elisha what are we going to do?" Elisha responded with the famous phrase, **"There are more with us, than there are with them.**" "Where," the servant undoubtedly screamed?

Elisha prayed: **Open this man's eyes so that he can see!** God did, and the servant saw that hovering just above Ben-Hadad's huge army was **a massive "heavenly host of angel warriors" with flaming chariots of fire** just waiting for God's signal to them to crush Ben-Hadad's whole miserable army and deliver God's children out of their trouble!

> **Psalm 34:7: "The angel of the Lord encamps around those who fear Him, and <u>he rescues them</u>!"**

That verse clearly doesn't apply to just Elisha, or King David who wrote it! That applies to you and me, and we started applying that to each of our own lives in the last two chapters, along with these two phrases:

1) PRAYER replaces PANIC!

2) Prayer opens our eyes to God's spiritual reality!

- That is, by the way, **the real reality** as opposed to the **"fogged-up reality"** we fallen humans tend to live in! Our limited three dimensions, as compared to the five or six or seven+ dimensions that God lives in. *(We don't know how many but there sure are more than three!)*

160

I've often told the story of the lady who came up to me after church and asked if I'd seen the two angels standing behind me during the sermon. I responded with something like, "No I hadn't, but thanks for the heads-up."

Then a second lady who was new to me, and new to lady #1, came up to me and described what she'd seen during the sermon, and it was the exact same thing! Now I was listening!

In that unseen 4th or 5th dimension, if we could see all the angels who are "standing guard around us who fear God" on any Sunday morning, the seats and aisles of our churches might be too full to sit or walk in! We might have more "social distancing" issues than Covid-19 brought us!

But here is my probing question for each of us:

- How did Elisha know the angels were there?
- **Obviously Elisha's eyes had already been opened! When? How?**
- One would assume that Elisha's eyes would have at one time been clouded over, so that he would have been worrying his head off about having it sliced off by some Aramean soldier's sword!
- But instead, he was sleeping like a baby even though he knew the biggest threat of his life, and to his life, was amassing just outside his front door.
- Wouldn't you like to have the kind of faith that allows you to rest in total peace, in the face of extreme

crises and trauma **instead of descending into fearful panic?** *(Some do! Why? How?)*

———————————

Can we trace in Elisha's life, what forged him into such a calm spiritual warrior? Do we know when he figured out that "**the angels of the Lord were going to be encamping around him, to deliver him in times of trouble**"? Yes, actually we can!

It seems <u>Elisha</u> had made the decision to attach his life to the Biblical prophet <u>Elijah</u>.

- Elijah would not have been an impressive man to look at, at least by 21st century standards. If we saw him coming down the isle at the grocery store, we would probably, purposely step into the next aisle.

- He was not a man we would have tended to invite over for coffee and cookies.

- But it was what was inside Elijah's soul that has made him a familiar name to every Christian on the planet, 2800 years after he died.

Elijah and Elisha's entire life and ministry, as recorded in the Bible, would fit into an area *(in my state of Florida)* between Melbourne to Fort Lauderdale, and from the Atlantic Ocean west to Lake Okeechobee in the middle of our state.

Both of them, almost certainly, still thought the world was flat! They had no idea that there was another whole side to a round planet, and that people like us, living on the other side of the world, would one day be talking about their lives!

162

But they came to know God, and experienced the power of God, in and through their lives, in an intense way that many modern God followers can't even imagine!

Elijah and Elisha walked everywhere they went in their tiny piece of the world. They knew little about what was going on 300 miles beyond the postage stamp size piece of real estate they lived on. And yet in just a few pages of Scripture,

- Elijah caused a widow's barrel of grain, and jar of cooking oil, to continue to pour out for months after it was empty.
- Elijah, through prayer, shut off rain, at least in his region of the world, for 3 ½ years!
- He, on two occasions, called down fire from heaven to make a spiritual point!
- He raised a dead boy back to life! *(There were sixteen miracles that we know of.)*

More importantly to our focus today, he started prophet schools in several locations around Israel and would apparently teach at one, then move on to the next, and the next.

Somewhere along the line a young man named Elisha came to hear him teach, began to watch him minister, saw his miracles, and God laid a call on his own life.

Elisha was *(tradition says)* the son of Shaphat, a wealthy land owner in Israel. There were undoubtedly other things he could have done with his life besides follow an odd-looking hermit around the country, but there was far more at stake here than filling empty oil jars.

Israel was being led by the wicked King Ahab and Queen Jezebel. They had fallen into the trap of embracing Jezebel's Baal gods. The Children of Israel said they still worshipped Yahweh, the Creator God of their ancestors, but they still found time for all the sexual perversion and child sacrificing that came with the worship of the Baal's.

So, Elijah forced the issue. His prayers shut off the rain for 40 long months, and finally he demanded a showdown on Mount Carmel. Jezebel's 450 prophets of Baal called on their gods to send fire to consume their sacrifice, while Elijah mocked them. They got nothing! They got zip from their worthless idols!

Then Elijah called on the one true God. A bolt of fire fell from heaven and consumed the sacrifice he had prepared for Almighty God. The Israelites once again turned a little bit, a "smidgin," of their attention and worship toward the God of their fathers.

Young Elisha so much wanted that for his life. No amount of money and influence could replace having an intense relationship with the Creator God of the Universe! And we find that intensity building into Elisha right up until the last day Elijah is alive on this earth. <u>Elisha is right there beside Elijah, on purpose</u>! This is a big deal!

The prophet Elijah knows that it is his last day on earth. Elisha also knows it is his mentor's last day on earth. The young students at the various "schools of the prophets" know it too.

What would you do if you knew it was your last day on this planet? If you knew for sure that you had less than 24 hours left to live, where would you go, who would you talk to? What would you say with your last few words?

We don't know that Elijah knew exactly what was going to happen. Perhaps he thought he was going to die of a massive heart attack. But that sure didn't stop him from getting his final day of exercise.

He starts in Samaria, and walks to the school of the prophets in Gilgal. The school dismisses classes, and they all gather around Elijah and Elisha **because Elisha won't leave his side!**

He then walks to the school in Bethel, then down to Jericho. Then he walks back up to the mountains of his home turf, a distance of 55 miles. **On his last day on earth he walks 55 miles,** with Elisha right there at his side, talking with an entourage of young prophet students!

> **2 Kings 2:2-4:** "And Elijah said to Elisha, 'Stay here, for the LORD has told me to go to Bethel.' But Elisha replied, 'As surely as the LORD lives and you yourself live, I will never leave you!' So they went down together to Bethel. The group of prophets from Bethel came to Elisha and asked him, 'Did you know that the LORD is going to take your master away from you today?' 'Of course I know,' Elisha answered. 'But be quiet about it.' Then Elijah said

to Elisha, 'Stay here, for the LORD has told me to go to Jericho.' But Elisha replied again, 'As surely as the LORD lives and you yourself live, I will never leave you.' So they went on together to Jericho..."

That same story keeps getting repeated. They arrive at the next school and Elijah encourages the students. Those prophet cadets get Elisha aside and say, "You know this is the Old Man's last day on earth, right?" And Elisha says, "Yes, now shut up!"

More than four dozen of the Cadet Prophets leave their schools and follow from a distance. They obviously want to know what is going to happen. Who else on the planet can predict the day of their death? And why does Elisha get to be the one who is standing at Elijah's elbow when he breathes his last breath? This was going to be interesting!

2 Kings 2:7-8: "Fifty men from the group of prophets also went and watched from a distance as Elijah and Elisha stopped beside the Jordan River. Then Elijah folded his cloak together and struck the water with it. The river divided, and the two of them went across on dry ground!"

- This makes a great children's story. But it was not recorded to be a children's story! Elijah has only a few minutes left on the planet.

- Elijah had spent his last few hours doing what he considered his most important final task – building up the Junior Prophets who would carry his torch once he was gone.

- He's very aware that Elisha is stuck to him like glue. He knows there are a whole gaggle of others watching them both from behind the trees. It's a bit hard to hide from him. He is a prophet after all! **He sees the unseen!**

Remember the low spiritual state Israel was in. Elijah has poured out his whole life trying to yank Israel out of their fascination with the hideous paganism and idolatry. He's now minutes away from leaving the planet, and the job is far from done! Once he's gone, the task of bringing salvation to Israel is going to be up to Elisha, up to those fifty gawking prophets, and the people they would teach, and the people who those people would then teach.

Elijah's "water swat" with his mantle wasn't because he didn't want to get his feet wet. He could have gone to the shallows and crossed the river like he had many times before! *(This isn't the mighty Mississippi!)*

I've been in that river. *(I'm sure some of you have too.)* It's not hard to cross except at flood stage. For that matter; Elijah could have simply gone straight to heaven from the Israel side of the river. Why cross it at all?

He's trying to leave a final vivid picture in all of their minds of the power of God, and **how much God can and will do through the life that is completely committed to him!**

We know who is watching the most intently of them all. **It's Elisha**! His heart is pounding as he watches Elijah take off his mantle. He see's his mentor lift it high into the air. He watches it come crashing down on the Jordan, water spraying everywhere. Then Elisha waits, holding his breath, until he sees the water begin to part from one side to the other just as Moses had parted the Red Sea.

We know what a big deal this was in the mind and heart of Elisha because of what happens immediately after.

- Any thoughts that Elisha is full of confidence are dead wrong. *(IMO)*

- Much like Moses did with General Joshua, telling him over and over not to be afraid, to be courageous. This is Elijah's way of showing Elisha that the power of God is greater than the power of the Baals or his misguided Jewish Queen.

- Elisha has an "inkling" that when he returns from this trip the job of taking on idolatry is going to land squarely on his shoulders.

- Elisha must have paused, scared, maybe terrified, praying in his heart:

"God, I'm not up to the task ahead!"
God is probably assuring him,
"Oh yes you are!"

<u>Probing Question #1:</u> If the generation following us is depending on our close walk with God to show them how to live out their lives, is there enough of God's presence and power in our lives to point the way?

<u>Probing Question #2:</u> If the generation following us is going to have an even tougher time than us fighting back the forces of darkness that are descending on our nation and world, is there enough of God's mighty power showing up in our lives to guide them? Are we so "calling down the power of heaven" on what is happening around us that the next generation is watching us saying, "Oh, now I see how to move forward empowered by the Almighty!"

<u>Probing Question #3:</u> If we know the next generation is going to have to be the salvation of our country and world, how serious are we about investing in them everything that God has built into us? And then showing them the pathway to become far more of a spiritual dynamo than we ever became in our own generation?

Elijah knows full well, there is one more thing he has to do before whatever brings him to his end on the earth. And Elisha knows with all his heart that there is going to have to be a transfer of God's "anointing," if he is going to have any chance at all of facing down the paganism.

I'm imagining that Elisha is wondering how in the world to broach the subject. He knows the sun is moving across the sky and one of these coming minutes, it's going to be too late. Turns out, Elijah starts the conversation. These are literally his last words. Imagine your last words as you pass your mantle to those who will pick it up and use it!

> **2 Kings 2:9: "When they came to the other side, Elijah said to Elisha, 'Tell me what I can do for you before I am taken away.' And Elisha replied, 'Please let me inherit a double share of your spirit and become your successor.'"**

Probing Question #4: What would be the effect if every one of us who have been growing in our faith for more than a few years would fix our eyes on a few of the next generation and ask the eternal question: "Tell me what I can do for you before I am taken away?"

- We're not talking here about leaving behind money or possessions. We're talking about the presence and the power of God being so evident, so measurable, so transferable in our lives, that the younger generations will wrestle their eyes away from the pagan things of this world and long to know God like we do!!

Some have suggested that Elisha was being greedy and self-serving, he wasn't! The firstborn Israelite received a double portion of his father's inheritance. Elisha wasn't Elijah's genetic firstborn, and he wasn't asking for his earthly possessions. He was Elijah's spiritual son. He knew if he didn't receive an outpouring of the same power of God, in even greater measure - (shenayim)

Father, Let a special measure of your spirit be on me

than Elijah experienced it, he would be swamped by what he was going to have to face when he got back on the other side of the Jordan.

He needed the same spirit Elijah had when he took on King Ahab, Queen Jezebel and the 450 prophets of Baal. Things were actually going to get worse for Israel before they got better, and he knew it. He was a prophet!

- "You've asked me for a difficult thing," Elijah said, not because he didn't want all that he was to be invested in Elisha.

- Not because he didn't want that to be his last earthly act, *(with all his heart he wanted that,)* but simply because it wasn't his gift to give. It was God's gift to give!

- If you see me when I am taken from you it will be yours, otherwise it will not!" *(2 Kings 2:10)*

"As they were walking along talking together *(and can't you just imagine that conversation)*, **suddenly a chariot of fire appeared, drawn by horses of fire. It drove between the two men, separating them, and Elijah was carried by a whirlwind into heaven. Elisha saw it and cried out, 'My father! My father! I see the chariots and charioteers of Israel!'** *(They weren't Israelites, they were angels, protectors of Israel.)* **And as they disappeared from sight, Elisha tore his clothes in distress."** *(2 Kings 2:11-12)*

We tend to get all focused on the spectacular departure, but verse 12 is maybe more important. Elisha saw all this unfold!

- All fifty of the prophet gawkers saw Elijah disappear. But there is no evidence that they saw why he disappeared, or they wouldn't have sent out a search team for three days trying to find him later in the chapter.
- **Elijah had said, "If you see me leave!"**

Clearly there is seeing and there is seeing!
If you see me with, not just your eyes,
but "the eyes of your heart"!

It is possible to have 20/20 vision on the outside and be totally blind on the inside! How many of us know people who live 80-90 years with good temporal vision, but they are totally blind to spiritual reality?

- That's why Paul in **Ephesians 1:18, prays "that the eyes of our heart will be opened."**

"By faith he (Moses) left Egypt, not fearing the King's anger. He persevered because He saw him who is invisible!" *(Hebrews 11:27)*

Hebrews 11:27 uses a phrase that helps us understand this principle. Moses was willing to leave the riches of Egypt to live in the wildness with the nomadic Hebrews because he "saw him who is invisible." How did Moses see an invisible God? By Faith!! Moses' faith gave him spiritual sight!

- **Faith sees what is really there – even though others see nothing at all!**

- Faith believes what is true – even when others remain totally unconvinced!

- By faith we are able to see what is really real!

- Amazing grace how sweet the sound that saved a wretch like me, I once was lost but now I'm found. <u>I once was blind, but now I see</u>!

"If you see me depart," Elijah said, you will get your request! What he meant was; your eyes will be opened and you will finally see the eternal!

- o And they were, and he did!

- o The other 50 just saw Elijah disappear but…

- o Elisha saw the angels of God swooping down in their chariots of fire to pick up Elijah and take him straight to heaven.

We know just how real this all became to Elisha, not just because he gathered up Elijah's mantle and smacked the waters of the Jordan and it rolled back for him as well. We know it because of what happened in Dothan. King Ben-Hadad's army didn't stand a chance because Elisha's vision was no longer earthly. When he saw Ben-Hadad's army gathering back in Aram, Elisha just looked up a little higher and there the vast army of Almighty God waiting for orders to crush the Arameans like cockroaches.

<u>Probing question # 5</u>: Has God begun to open our spiritual eyes, until we aren't just viewing this world through earthly temporal fallen eyes, but we are starting (by the grace of God) to be able to look beyond the "visible" and see the mighty power of God arrayed to protect ourselves, our

families, our communities, our state, our nation, and our world?

2 Kings 2:13-15: "**Elisha picked up Elijah's cloak, which had fallen when he was taken up. Then Elisha returned to the bank of the Jordan River. He struck the water with Elijah's cloak and cried out, 'Where is the LORD, the God of Elijah?' Then the river divided, and Elisha went across. When the group of prophets from Jericho saw from a distance what happened, they exclaimed, 'Elijah's spirit rests upon Elisha!' And they went to meet him and bowed to the ground before him.**"

- Can't you imagine the level of trepidation in Elisha as he walks up to that Jordan River?
- He knew he had fifty prophets watching to see if Elijah's spirit was now resting on him. He knew he could not simply wade across the Jordan.
- He had absolutely no choice but to walk up to the water's edge and yell; **"Where is the Lord God of Elijah?"**
- And then he waited! And then the first little wave left the shore, and then the whole Jordan rolled back just like it had for Elijah, and the Red Sea had for Moses.

In our own modern lives, we might be saying phrases like:

1) Where is the Lord God of Billy Sunday?

2) Where is the Lord God of D. L. Moody?

3) Where is the Lord God of Jim Elliot?

174

But I promise you there is a more important question that needs to be asked in the days to come, when we come to our final breath.

<u>Probing question #6:</u> **Who will pick up your mantle and say, "Where is the Lord God of _____."** Who will pick up my mantle and say "Where is the Lord God of Sam Chess?"

Forty years ago, I attended the funeral of my grandfather **Glenn Chess**. He was a man who cast a very long shadow. At his viewing the waiting line extended out of the funeral home and down the sidewalk along the street.

I sat in the third row in the church building, a church that he *(as an engineer)* had helped plant. A minister told the story of Elijah and Elisha. He then asked a question that rocked my world. **Who will pick up the mantle of Glenn Chess? Is there an Elisha in the room that will say, "I'll take his mantle?"**

I have no idea what anybody else in the room was thinking but I vividly remember a raw ball of emotion rising in my chest. **"<u>I will</u>," I screamed on the inside.** Eight years later I planted a church just like my grandfather had. *(It was Grace Emmanuel Church, where I still pastor today – 31 years later.)*

But as time progressed and my own hair turned from dark to gray, a question began to increasingly hammer into my mind. I need it to hammer into your minds as well, as you read these final pages:

*Who in the world would pick
up my mantle one day?*

Who would want to?

Who will pick up yours?

- Is there enough of God's presence and power in my life that someone, anyone, would want to say: "I want that same power and presence in my own life!"
- Let's just say there is! Let's just say we do have those coming behind us who are watching our lives and saying, "I want what he/she has!"
- If they pick up our mantle, will they walk up to the Jordan River of their lives with all of their peers watching?
- Will they wrap our mantle up into a club and smack the Jordan River of their lives saying:

Where is the Lord God of _____?

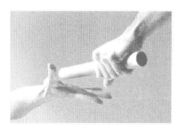

Will they have the faith to see the water cascade back because of what they learned about God from us? *(Elisha has twice as many miracles recorded in the Bible as Elijah did!)*

o Will the people we are passing the race baton to, be able to run up alongside us in the relay we call life?

- Will we get the baton into their hands without dropping it?

- Will they then take off on the same race we have shown them how to run?

- Will they run it even faster and more accurately than we did because they will be asking **"Where is the Lord God of _____ (me/you)?"**

- Because the Almighty God of _____ *(you/me)* has already shown up hugely, in their lives?

Dedication – The Rest of the Story

I shared with you something of the difficult time I was faced with in 2020. It was physical, it was mental, it was emotional. It was far worse than I will ever share. And it was already in full swing long before Covid crashed into our world. In desperation I called from my walk around the pond to my friend **Dr. Walter Barron.**

And he pulled on the power of heaven and took on the forces of hell like I've already described.

I told you of getting back to my truck and pouring out pages and pages of words from God onto the paper… just as fast as my pen would write, another sentence came!

I started a series of sermons at Grace Emmanuel Church that next week called "What Scares Demons" based on what God was teaching me…and that's now the content of this book.

I also wrote a prayer for myself, during that time, and I called it "MY WAR PRAYER." It was very personal. I'm now going to share it with you.

Amazingly, when I sensed satan turning his machine gun of harassment on in my life – I found/find that the praying of this prayer really did/does push back the powers of darkness.

- When I began to pray this WAR Prayer I sensed the evil one saying to me, "You pray that prayer and I'm going to come after you even harder!"

- My response was; "When you come after me harder… *you can't come one step closer than my Heavenly Father allows* … and **I promise you, I will respond by teaching more and more people how to effectively fight back against you!"**

- **That's what I am doing right now!**

I shared this story with our Church on January 10, 2021. What I didn't tell them was that the night before my wife and I were standing in the parking lot of the Covid-filled hospital near our home with several more friends and family – and my pastor friend Walter was lying in a bed in the ICU deathly sick.

We called on heaven to preserve his life, because so many still so needed his prayers! The nurses turned him so he could see us all out in the parking lot calling on God.

And I turned and looked just across the street to the sidewalk around the Tradition Lake where his prayer had so impacted my life.

- **Three weeks later – Pastor Walter Barron died**!

- I stood by his casket and **I asked God to give me a portion of his spirit,** like Elisha did with Elijah.

- His legacy lives on in this book and in the prayer I'm going to share with you now:

<u>My War Prayer</u> !

1) Jesus I come to you so thankful for how you have worked out your grace in my life. I'm so thankful for how you have used my life in eternal ways in the past and are in the process of using it in even greater ways.

2) I'm thankful for the healing power (physical, mental, and spiritual) that you have brought into my body, my mind, and my soul. I am living in and through the power of Jesus – brought about through your victorious death and resurrection!

3) Satan continues to try one avenue after another to convince me that God's grace is not sufficient for me, that I am too weak to resist his advances – but he is lying. He always lies! He can't not lie, even to himself!

4) Satan, I have been promised by God in James 4:7 that:

- If I submit myself to my Heavenly Father
- And if I resist you and push back against your forces of darkness
- That you will be forced to flee from me!

5) So right now I, once again, submit myself to the power and presence and protection of Almighty God!

6) I instruct you, satan, to "flee" from my life, and from the lives of all those God has connected to me! I direct that you must "flee" through the power of Jesus' death on the cross, through my Savior's total defeat of your "temporary kingdom of darkness" by his resurrection from the dead!

7) I instruct through the power of my risen Savior that the demons that you have assigned to me today be paralyzed in their effort to attack and harass me and my _____!

- I submit them under the power of Jesus' atoning death and his victorious, triumphant resurrection.
- I ask that satan's evil minions be paralyzed in their attempts, and that they be eternally assigned, forever, to the "lake of fire"!

ACKNOWLEDGEMENTS

God nudged **Cass Everett**, after her retirement, to sell her home in Pennsylvania and move to the 'unknown land' of South Florida. In God's providential plan she ended up just a few miles from our church. Cass' use of her spiritual gifts has become invaluable at Grace Emmanuel Church, but she has become, to me, a gift from God.

Who, but God, could have planned an ADD pastor linking up with a gentle "do it by the book" editor. This book literally would not have been in print without the time Cass has invested in it.

She has poured so, so many long hours into repeatedly editing and reviewing and re-editing the manuscripts for this book and for "Unmasking Revelation." No one but God will ever know the long evenings she sat up late into the night finding the phrase that didn't quite communicate, finding the exclamation mark before the quotation mark rather than after it, finding the underline extending under the period. She also tirelessly worked through the use of every Scripture, culminating in the Scripture index at the end of this book.

Penny Worley, the administrative secretary at Grace Emmanuel Church, designed the cover of this book. She is also a special gift from God in my life. In spite of the already huge demands on her time at the church, when I walk into Penny's office with a personal project, she never fails to give away her free time, and always with excellence beyond measure.

A special thanks to **Riva Alvarado** for her final proofread.

SCRIPTURE BY BOOK INDEX

Unless otherwise indicated, all Scripture quotations are taken from the Holy Bible, **New Living Translation,** copyright © 1996, 2004, 2015 by Tyndale House Foundation. Used by permission of Tyndale House Publishers, Inc., Carol Stream, Illinois 60188. All rights reserved.

Scripture Indexes compiled by Cass Everett.

SCRIPTURE BY CHAPTER INDEX

Additional Scripture Versions used:

ABOUT THE AUTHOR

Sam Chess has served as a Pastor on the Treasure Coast, of Florida, for more than 40 years. He serves as the Senior Pastor of Grace Emmanuel Church *(EFCA)* in Port Saint Lucie. *(graceemmanuel.com)* He and his wife Sue founded the church in 1990.

Grace Emmanuel has two radio programs called "GRACE ALIVE" on the regional Christian radio station WCNO. *(WCNO.com)* The, four times a week, program reaches from Ft. Lauderdale to Melbourne, FL, across much of the state, and into the Bahamas.

Sam serves on the board of the Treasure Coast Christian Alliance, which brings together local government officials, business leaders, and Church leaders in unity and purpose.

Sam and Sue have three grown children and nine wonderful grandchildren. Sue Chess serves as the Executive Director of Care Net Pregnancy Services of the Treasure Coast.

Sam holds a Bachelor's degree from Hobe Sound Bible College and a Master's degree from Trinity International University.

Sam is also the author of the book, *Unmasking Revelation*, published by Morgan James Publishing. (2020)

You can contact him at *sam@unmaskingrevelation.com* or *info@unmaskingrevelation.com.*, or at *samchess.com*